Managing Change and Development in Schools

Other titles in this series

Public Relations and Marketing for Schools
by Tim Devlin and Brian Knight

Designing The School Day by Brian Knight

Managing Change and Development in Schools

A Practical Handbook

by

John Elliott-Kemp and

Nicholas Elliott-Kemp

Longman School Management Resources

Published by Longman Industry and Public Service Management, Longman Group UK Limited, 6th Floor, Westgate House, The High, Harlow, Essex CM20 1YR, England
Telephone: Harlow (0279) 442601
Fax: Harlow (0279) 444501 Group 3 & 2

First published 1992

A catalogue record for this book is available from The British Library

ISBN 0-582-09342-2

Typeset by Communitype Communications Limited
164 Barkby Road, Leicester LE4 7LF
Printed by Page Bros, Norwich

C ontents

Introduction

In the last fifteen years the management of change and development in organisations has grown from a specialist minority interest into a field of central concern, not just for academics and theoreticians but for all who are involved in the management of organisations. This includes both those who are managers and those who are managed.

Our own professional experience has ranged from classroom teaching to school headship, and in higher education from Initial Teacher Training to In-Service programmes for staff at all levels of work in schools and colleges. Our prime interest is consequently in the management of change and development in educational organisations. During the period of our working lives we have witnessed an enormous shift of emphasis in the management of schools. This has amounted to a sea-change, from managing a relatively 'steady state' in a world of fairly regular and predictable developments, dramas and crises, to one where there is very little ground on which to stand. This is now a world where change has become the norm rather than the exception, the foreground rather than the background of school life. And while a school staff will be continually involved in change and development initiatives, not all of these will be of their own choosing.

As far as anyone can predict there will never be a period of stability again when one will have the luxury of time to reflect, consolidate progress and take stock of the situation in a more leisurely manner. All our practical experience seems to confirm the warning notes sounded by economists and organisation and management scholars that the world has lost its 'stable state' (Schon, 1971) and we are now in an age of discontinuity (Drucker, 1969) in which change is so rapid and turbulent as to induce 'future shock' (Toffler, 1970), where our present lives are invaded by the future in the form of powerful, accelerative thrusts of change.

Too many changes in too short a time can cause shattering stress and disorientation and consequent loss of effectiveness. How are schools and colleges to face this challenge of continual change? It seems that a new kind of teacher, a new kind of leader and a new kind of school are needed for the last decade of the twentieth century, and that training for change and development must be given high priority. The goal of such training would be to help us to learn to cope more effectively with personal and social change in our professional lives and to manage the processes of educational change and development in our schools and colleges.

Our purpose in producing this practical manual is to provide resource materials to assist schools in their In-Service training in the management of change and development. It will also be useful for those who provide training programmes within Local Education Authorities, in universities or polytechnics, or as freelance trainers. All the exercises and instruments in this book have been piloted in our own training and consultancy programmes for schools, colleges and management trainers in the UK and overseas[1].

We have chosen to organise the book around three major integrating concepts – the Organisational Context, the Innovation or Change and the Change Agent Group responsible for the change. Within each of these major chapter headings is a collection of practical exercises and instruments designed to help a school staff to become active agents of worthwhile change and development. Our vision of the school preparing to meet the demands of the 1990s is that of a self-renewing organisation – one which is continually re-examining its role and its achievement, where staff prepare themselves and their students to face the challenges of tomorrow rather than strive to address the problems of yesterday.

But one can never have a self-renewing school without self-renewing people. The emphasis in the book is therefore on people and their growth and development, whatever their position or role in the school.

There is no 'ideal' sequence in approaching the different sections of the book, rather a number of possible 'routes'. Some of the alternative routes are as follows:

— a school could start with either of the major sections in the 'Organisational Context' and as a result of the chosen diagnostic exercise identify a development project. Before initiating the change, relevant parts of the chapters on the Change Agent Group and on the Innovation or Change could be used to prepare staff to implement the change and ensure that it is well managed.

— a school might decide to undertake a comprehensive change agent training programme for all, or selected groups of staff. Chapter 2 (the Change Agent Group) is then used as the core resource and the training programme takes staff systematically through this chapter, drawing on other sections of the book when a specific innovation is planned by the group.

— a school may have the task of implementing a change which is not necessarily of its own choice, for example a new mandatory requirement from central government or a recommendation by the inspectorate following a review or inspection of the school. In this example the most relevant sections are likely to be the Change Agent Inventory (Chapter 2), the EPIC exercise for exploring staff perceptions and the sections in Chapter 4 on analysing innovations.

We should like to express our thanks to all our client schools and colleges for giving us the opportunity to pilot the exercises in the book and providing suggestions for improvement. Amongst these clients we are especially grateful to the Bradford, Clevelend, Cheshire, Leeds and London schools we have worked with, to the schools of the English Schools Foundation, Hong Kong, and the National Institute for Development of Educational Administrators in Thailand.

Finally, we should like to acknowledge the co-operation of Monica Moseley, Administrator of PAVIC Publications, Sheffield City Polytechnic, for permission to reproduce items from the SIGMA school development project, and to Ann Rickards who was responsible for the typing of the manuscript.

Note

[1] Helios International and SIGMA consultancy are based at Helios House, 82 Dore Road, Sheffield, and PAVIC Publications, Sheffield City Polytechnic, UK.

References

DRUCKER, P. (1969) *The Age of Discontinuity*, Pan Books.
SCHON, D. (1971) *Beyond the Stable State*, Temple Smith.
TOFFLER, A. (1970) *Future Shock*, Bodley Head.

The key variables and the change process

In this chapter we shall begin to explore the concepts of 'leadership', 'management', 'change agent' and 'organisation'. Effective leadership has always been an important factor in achieving change. But anyone can perform a leadership role: the right to lead is not the exclusive prerogative of head-teachers or principals. One may be a formally appointed leader whose role may involve responsibility for leading a specific group of staff or a whole school. Or one may be a main-scale teacher who perceives a need within the school, convinces colleagues of that need at a staff meeting and helps mobilise staff energy and commitment to carry out appropriate change.

An allied concept to that of 'leader' is the role of 'agent of change'. A change agent is a person who undertakes the task of changing or developing some aspect of a system or organisation. The change agent may work alone, but more likely as a member of a change agent team. Being a change agent implies a conscious commitment to purposeful change – to making things happen rather than just allowing them to drift. All teachers are therefore change agents, for teaching can be defined as a purposive activity aimed at facilitating and managing the achievement of worthwhile change and development in students (ie learning).

Leadership and management

During the 1980s there has been considerable debate on the relationship between 'management' and 'leader-ship'. The prevailing consensus in 1990 appears to be as follows:

Management has evolved in terms of certain key processes or techniques. These processes tend to be rational or scientific in their basic assumptions and values and are believed by practitioners to be applicable to the whole range of organisational settings.

The following processes are listed as key elements in management in virtually all contemporary analyses –

1. *Goal setting,* as in 'Management by Objectives' (MBO).
2. *Planning:* the processes and specific techniques needed to move the organisation towards its goals, ie the means of achieving ends.
3. *Budgeting and resource management.* This is that aspect of planning concerned with the finances of the organisation and includes the acquisition and utilisation of resources.
4. *Organising:* setting up the structures necessary to facilitate the realisation of plans, appointing people to specific roles within the structure, devolving authority and creating career and reward systems to motivate people appropriately.
5. *Controlling.* This is concerned with the monitoring of activities, processes and outcomes to ensure that everything is on course and 'according to plan'. Corrective mechanisms, review systems and financial controls are examples falling under this heading.

Leadership, although a concept which in some aspects overlaps the concept of management, contains certain elements which emphasise its distinctiveness. The present consensus can be summarised thus:

1. *Sensing* a need to adapt or change. Effective leaders can identify the key areas where the organisation must respond to a turbulent environment *before* the need becomes so urgent that it takes on the proportions of a crisis.

   This 'sensing' skill is part intuitive, part information-based. It requires the ability to process information about the environment and create radical new solutions or ideas which are independent of the past, often breaking the mould of past problem-solving methods. We can assess the importance of sensing ability in rational management terms by means of a cost-benefit diagram as seen in Figure 1.1.

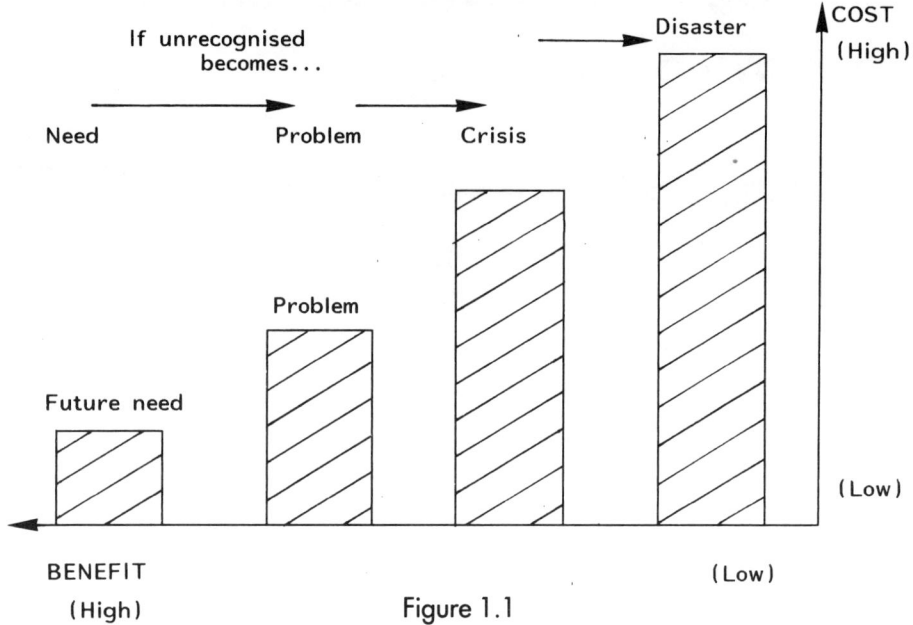

Figure 1.1

A need which is not sensed and acted upon appropriately becomes a problem which will demand greater resources (people, time, energy, money) in order to solve it.

A problem unrecognised and unsolved in time becomes a crisis, which consumes even more resources.

A crisis not acted upon promptly and effectively becomes a disaster which could possibly overwhelm or ruin the organisation.

The leader's ability to sense future needs, particularly in strategic issues, is therefore a key skill.

2. *Envisioning.* It is not enough simply to identify a set of key needs for the organisation's future. The effective leader must be able to create, with colleagues, a bold new vision of the organisation and its mission when it is responding to those key needs.

    An essential part of this 'envisioning' process involves actually picturing in the mind what the future state of the organisation will be, together with a clear, positive view of the part that everyone will need to play in realising the vision. This last requirement will inevitably involve a great deal of interaction with colleagues, for they are unlikely to have a sense of ownership of the vision and give it their wholehearted commitment unless they have been involved in the envisioning process and perceive their leader as one who is sensitive to their legitimate needs and interests.

3. *Enacting.* Where the envisioning stage is concerned with creation and communication of a vision of the organisation's future, this 'enacting' stage in leadership involves the turning of the vision into reality.

    'Enacting' for the leader must entail modelling the values, processes and behaviours consistent with the vision. Without this positive model of the vision on the leader's part the rest of the organisation cannot be expected to attain the vision. Other aspects of the 'enacting' phase involve the practical strategies for implementation such as the development of teams, task forces and networks necessary to maintain the high energy levels for radical change and innovation, together with the creation of a culture appropriate to creativity and development.

To summarise: effective leadership, as distinct from management, involves need sensing, envisioning and enacting. This means creating an appropriate agenda for change, including a clear vision of the future and the development of implementation teams and networks.

It can be readily seen that management courses, whether short training programmes or Masters' degree programmes, teach management concepts, methods and techniques. But they do not teach leadership. The best alumni of the management colleges become effective managers or administrators, not leaders.
One may, of course, learn all about leadership without becoming an effective leader. One may simply be good at talking about leadership. But learning to lead means learning to walk as you talk. Leadership is practised in deeds and attitudes more than in words.
This work can never guarantee that you will become an effective leader, therefore. It may help you to become more articulate in conceptualising and communicating the nature of leadership. It may help you to develop action plans for leadership. But in the end, only you can actually put into practice the ideas and precepts necessary for effective leadership.

Bibliography
Amongst the many recent works on leadership, including its relationship to management, we have found the following amongst the most useful:

BENNIS, W. and NANUS, B. (1986) *Leaders,* Harper & Row.
DEMING, W. (1986) *Out of the Crisis,* Cambridge University Press.
HANDY, C. (1989) *The Age of Unreason,* Hutchinson.
HARVEY-JONES, J. (1988) *Making It Happen: Reflections on Leadership,* Collins.
HUNT, J. G. *et al* (eds) (1984) *Leaders and Managers,* Pergamon Press.
KOTTER, J. P. (1988) *The Leadership Factor,* The Free Press.
PETERS, T. (1987) *Thriving on Chaos,* Harper & Row.
TICHY, N. and DEVANNA, M. (1986) *The Transformational Leader,* John Wiley.

Management and leadership: the ALAMO hypothesis
The acronym 'ALAMO' stands for 'Appropriate Leadership and Management Orientation'. The ALAMO thesis is that 'management' and 'leadership' are complementary concepts. The relation between the two concepts appears to be similar to the 'Yin–Yang' polarity used in Taoism (see Figure 1.2).

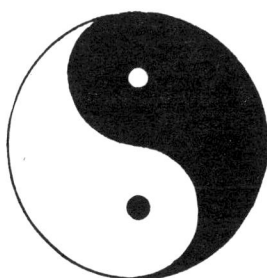

Figure 1.2

In Taoism, the universe is seen as being in permanent flux and change. The precise balance between Yin and Yang will therefore need to change over time. The key factor influencing the balance of leadership and management (Yin and Yang) is the environment, especially the extent to which it is characterised by relative stability and predictability, or by rapid, turbulent and discontinuous change.
As in the Yin–Yang, it is never an 'either–or' choice but a question of *relative emphasis* during a given period.

The ALAMO hypothesis can be visualised in the form of a 'U' tube model as seen in Figure 1.3.

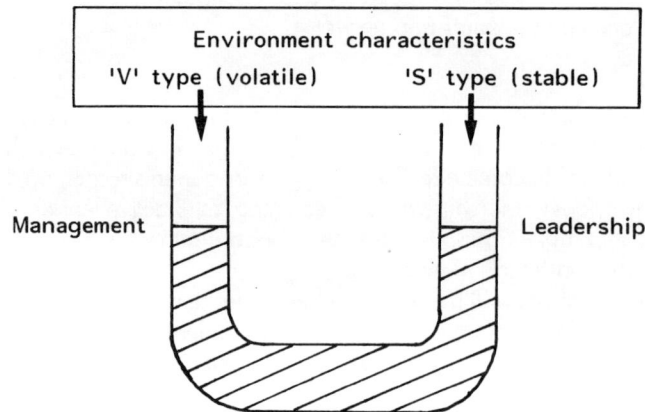

Figure 1.3

An Appropriate Management and Leadership Orientation (ALAMO) is that which is in accord with the characteristics of the environment:

The 'S' type environment is one where there is a period of stability. Changes are relatively slow, and tend to be developmental, that is to say continuities of existing trends. Consequently, it is an environment where one can predict needs and contingencies and plan accordingly.

In an 'S' type environment the processes of management are of central importance, and the emphasis will need to be on 'administrative' factors (keeping things going), rather than on 'dynamic' factors (innovation and leadership).

This can be illustrated in the ALAMO 'U' tube model (see Figure 1.4).

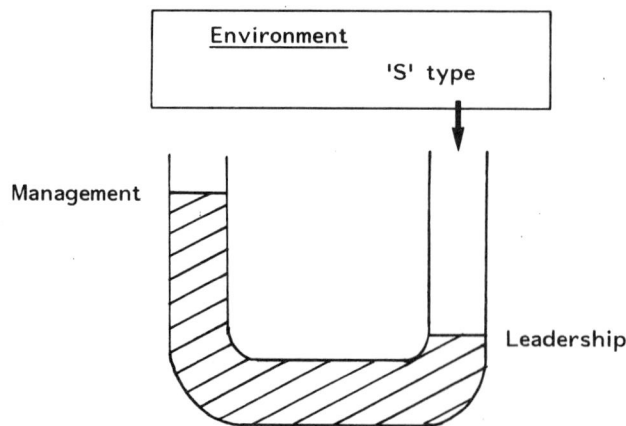

Figure 1.4

The 'V' type environment (see Figure 1.5) is characterised by its volatile nature. Not only is there constant change, but this change is rapid, far exceeding any previous rate of environmental change, and involving changes of great magnitude.

The volatile environment produces few continuities: it is an era of discontinuity, making a nonsense of any attempts at long-term planning or prediction.

A 'tight' management system, emphasising structure, bureaucratic reliance on job descriptions and close monitoring and control is inappropriate in a volatile world. Rigid systems result in an inability to respond to new challenges or crises, innovative ideas are often discouraged in favour of a climate of 'dynamic conservatism' which makes maintenance of the status quo a top priority.

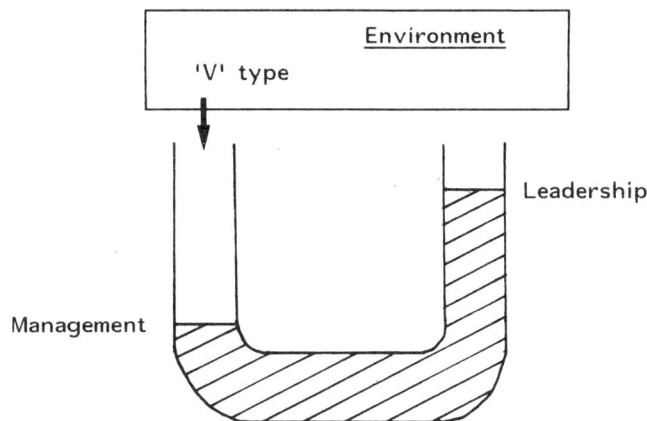

Figure 1.5

In a 'V' type environment the linear, rational processes of traditional 'Yang' management seem to be less appropriate than the relatively intuitive 'Yin' concept of leadership. In this situation the need is for a clear vision, based on accurate need sensing, and backed by an adaptive structure based on task groups and implementation networks rather than bureaucratic models.

Organisations

A leader, manager or change agent usually operates in the context of an organisation, and will, therefore, need some understanding of the concept of organisation. There are many ways of conceptualising an organisation but the model that is easiest to grasp and apply is probably the one which follows. 'Models' in the sense used here are not 'real', but are simply mental constructs used as mindholds to help us grasp the basic essentials of a complex idea or problem.

All organisations will require four related sub-systems, clusters of tasks and activities linked to particular purposes.

1. The first sub-system can be termed the 'administrative' aspect of the organisation. Its function is to ensure that the organisation is 'ticking over' like a well-tuned engine and it is especially concerned with those aspects designed to produce a trouble-free state of orderliness and predictability, such as rules and regulations, standard procedures, prescribed roles and obligations.

    All organisations, whether a school or one of its component parts such as a classroom, rely on establishing this state of order as their foundation.

2. The second sub-system is the 'reactive' aspect of the organisation. This is concerned with the deployment of resources to meet and resolve a crisis. Whatever the crisis, whether it is a serious accident in the playground, a fire in the school kitchen or the threat of school closure, it will be essential to ensure swift action to deal with it. Since resources are finite this will inevitably mean that time and energy are drained from other tasks.

3. The third sub-system, in contrast, is the proactive aspect of the organisation. Here, instead of simply reacting to events one is making things happen. The proactive sub-system is concerned with purposeful, planned change, that side of the organisation devoted to innovation, development and learning.

    We may visualise the organisation by putting these three sub-systems in the form of a triangle, with the administrative system acting as the base, or foundation, for the organisation (see Figure 1.6).

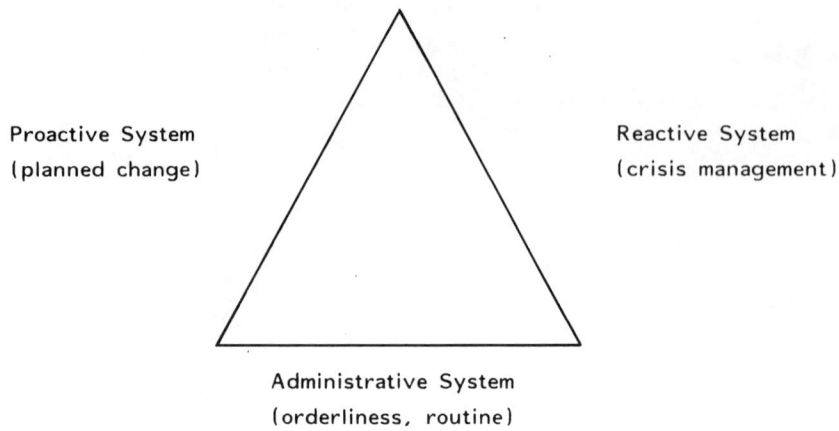

Proactive System
(planned change)

Reactive System
(crisis management)

Administrative System
(orderliness, routine)

Figure 1.6

Our organisational model as it stands is incomplete: it requires a further sub-system to enable it to become fully functional.

4.   The fourth sub-system is the co-ordinating function which pulls the system together and makes it an organic entity, capable of 'learning'. This co-ordinating function acts as a feedback loop from the proactive and reactive systems to the administrative system (see Figure 1.7).

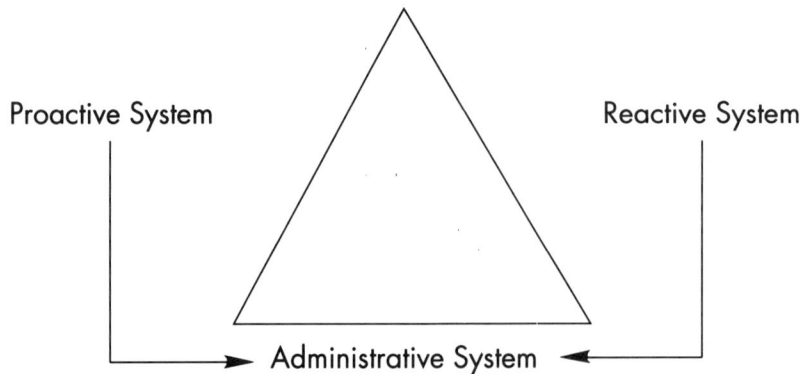

Proactive System

Reactive System

Administrative System

Figure 1.7

–   after a crisis has been dealt with it will be important to consider if it could ever occur again. If this is the case there will be a need to build standing instructions and procedures into the administrative system to meet this eventuality. It may also be necessary to conduct a training session to test the preparedness of the appropriate staff.

–   when innovation has been introduced it will be necessary to provide support systems to ensure that any problems are dealt with and the innovation becomes an integral part of the organisation. It will be important to take a long-term perspective and ensure that succession planning is not overlooked.

Many innovations fail to survive because the innovators move on and no-one has prepared staff to carry on the momentum of the change. Succession planning will involve a clear and coherent policy for staff development and in-service training.

An effective organisation will be one in which

- crises are not repeated because people learn from their experience,
- the administrative system provides an orderly and secure framework without smothering people in unnecessary regulations or paperwork,
- the greater part of people's time and energy is applied to managing change, development and learning.

The big difference between previous ages and our own is the *increasing* emphasis on the proactive side of the organisational triangle. Schools in the 1990s face change which is rapid, discontinuous, even turbulent. Sudden demands for change may provide little advance warning and are often unrelated to previous changes. These changes place demands on all staff. The implications of this are far-reaching for all those who work in schools:

- the only effective schools in the long term will be those which are self-renewing: taking charge of their own development, sensing future needs, acting on their diagnosis, carrying out their own reviewing and evaluation,
- to become a self-renewing school we must have staff who are self-renewing. This means that school staff will need to accept that managing change is everyone's business: every teacher, and everyone in a management role must learn to become an agent of change. Each individual then accepts the need for his/her own growth and development, for being a change agent begins with self-change. Each individual acts as a change agent to others in the form of influence on individual colleagues, working groups and school policy and practices.

The literature on organisations consistently emphasises that long-term organisational effectiveness depends on a healthy blend of both top-down (management-initiated) and bottom-up (grass roots) change. One of the central tasks of management in the 1990s will be to facilitate and co-ordinate these major thrusts for change to ensure a healthy growth in the organisation.

The aim of this book is to provide ideas and resource materials to help schools and their staff become self-renewing – schools in which each individual is an agent of worthwhile change.

Exercise

Being an agent of change implies first of all being in charge of your own change and development. It will be useful for your professional development to use the triangle model of an organisation to analyse your own work situation.

This can be done whatever your role or position: the challenge is to identify over a period of one week where your time and energy are channelled, using the format of a simple 'log book' at the end of each day.

The system is simple enough to be completed in five minutes per day, with an additional fifteen minutes at the end of the week to synthesise data and plan what to do in order to become more effective.

Effectiveness implies maximum time and energy being channelled into the left (proactive) side of the triangle, ensuring that feedback energy is used to 'update' or 'top up' the administrative system so that it has a memory to help deal with repeat problems.

The proactive system is therefore concerned with leadership and development, including the management and facilitation of learning.

Your daily log is best kept in the form of a single sheet for each day, as in the following example:

Day/date...................................		
Time	*Activities* (rough analysis)	*Categories*[1]
9.00-10.30		
11.00-12.30		
1.30- 3.30		

[1]*Key*   A – administrative

           R – reactive, or 'fire-fighting'

           P – proactive, managing development, learning or change

           C – co-ordinating (ensuring that crises or development 'hiccups' will be better managed next time)

Use the right-hand column to record your estimate of the percentage time spent on each category, eg –

A teacher:

    A – 15 (registration, giving out books, etc)

    R – 5 (dealing with miscreants)

    P – 75 (teaching/supervising students' work)

    C – 5 (laying down new rules for student conduct and for monitoring their future behaviour)

When reviewing the average percentage estimates for the whole week your goal will be to maximise the proactivity score by keeping the 'reactive' and 'administrative' scores at reasonable levels.

The key variables and the change process – overview of the book

In this section we shall map out the central concepts we shall be using in the book and relate these to the process of change management.

We shall use three organising concepts to construct the model framework:

Organisation — the organisational context for the change process (This could be a classroom, a department or work group, or a whole school system).

Innovation — the specific change to be undertaken including its purpose, characteristics and required resources.

Change agent group — the group of people whose task it is to implement the change (Although solitary change agents do exist, most significant changes are achieved by teamwork and consequently the first golden rule for any lone change agent must be 'Find your allies and create a team for change').

These three organising concepts can now be grouped in the form of a Venn diagram (see Figure 1.8).

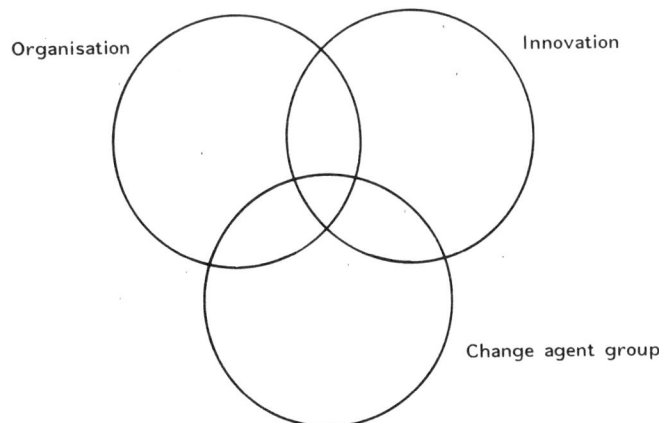

Figure 1.8

This can help us to clarify our thinking about the different areas of 'innovation', 'organisation' and 'change agent group' *in relation to each other*, and having achieved a 'mindhold' on the complexities of managing change we can then use the model as a springboard for action.

Each of the major circle areas will need to be explored and appropriate action taken. Succeeding chapters of this work will focus on these areas in turn and provide activities and guidelines to assist effective management of change.

Managing Organisational Change:

The Pre-implementation Phase

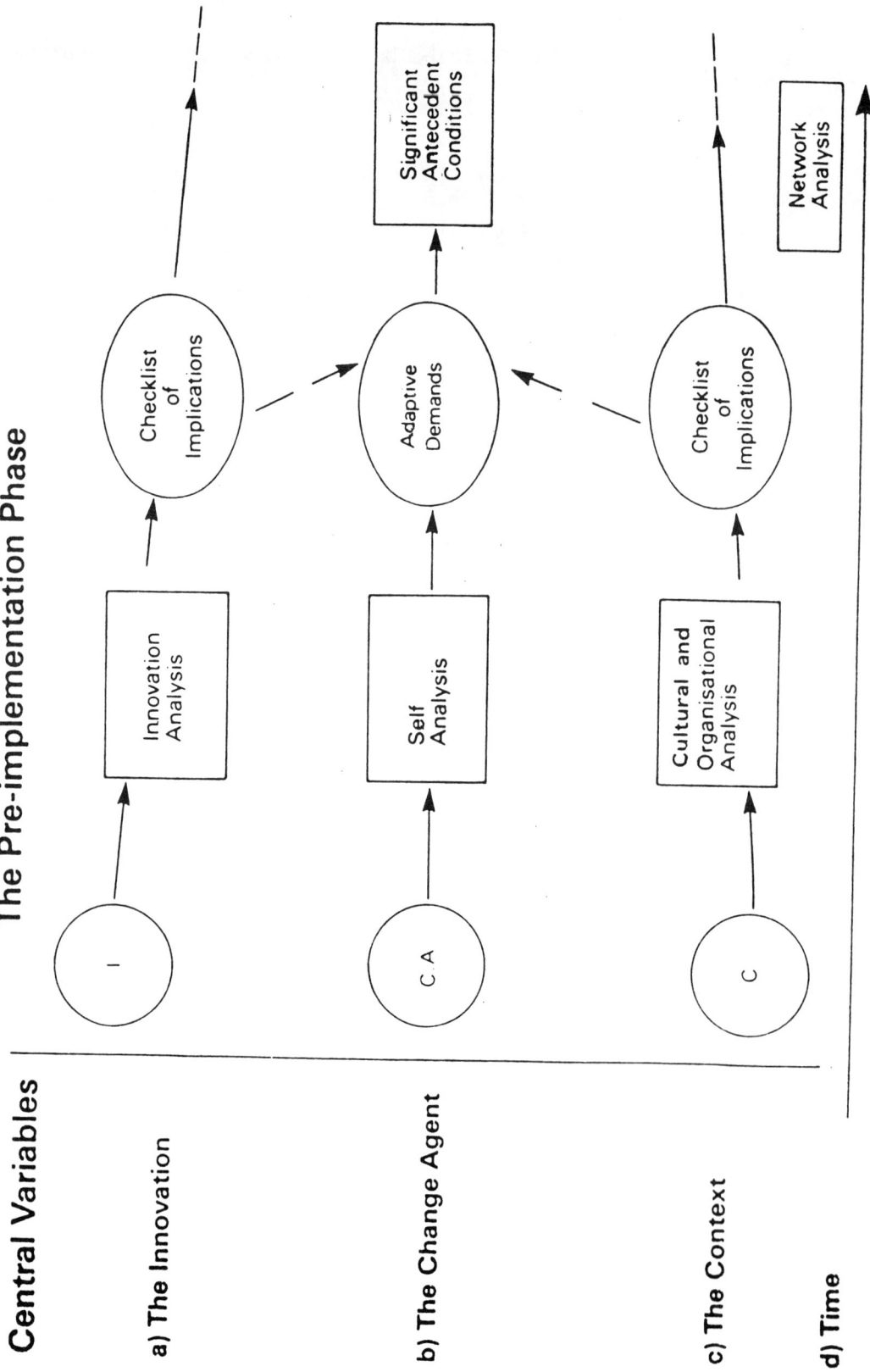

Central Variables

a) The Innovation

b) The Change Agent

c) The Context

d) Time

Innovation Analysis

Checklist of Implications

Self Analysis

Adaptive Demands

Significant Antecedent Conditions

Cultural and Organisational Analysis

Checklist of Implications

Network Analysis

© John Elliott-Kemp 1988
Helios International

Figure 1.9

Exercise

At this point it will be useful for readers to undertake a preliminary exercise using the model outlined. This will help to internalise the system and also raise some of the most important issues involved in managing change. You may select a particular innovation that you are intending to initiate in the near future, or, if you wish, use the case study method and look back at a change from your past experience.

Innovation
Describe the innovation.

What need does it fulfil?

What is its purpose?

What are its underlying values?

What is the source of the innovation?
(eg Who has chosen it? Who wants it?)

What extra resources are required?
(Include new knowledge and skills)

What time scale is envisaged?
(eg preparation and planning time, gradual introduction or school-wide implementation)

Organisation
Define the boundaries of the innovation
(eg whole school, year group).

Are the values and practices involved in the change congruent with existing values and practices?

Can you identify any areas where there is lack of congruence?

Are there any existing practices or enterprises to which the innovation could be linked?

Change agent group
Which members of staff will be responsible for implementing the change?

Do they have the necessary knowledge and skills?

How committed are they?

Are the necessary resources available?
(Include aspects such as time, teaching space, goodwill on the part of ancillary or domestic staff)

Is everyone clear about the purpose of the change and their role in it?

How will you measure success in this venture?

DATA ANALYSIS
When we have completed the questionnaire we are in a position to identify an agenda for the pre-implementation phase of innovation.
We are acknowledging that change is seldom an event, but more often a process. And this process requires thinking, discussion, planning and, above all, time.
The challenge, in our analysis of the data we have collected, is to identify the implications for us under each of the headings of

- organisational context,
- the innovation,
- the change agent group.

Finally, we shall need to synthesise our findings in the form of *significant antecedent conditions*.

What this involves is agreeing and listing all the things which must be done, arising from our responses to the list of questions, in order to ensure the success of the innovation.

The process we have followed can be set out in the form of a model of the pre-implementation phase (see Figure 1.9).

The more innovation and change can be viewed as a process, rather than an event, and the more we can learn to plan that process, the greater the chances of success. We must remember that failure for a change agent group may leave a legacy of low morale and reduced energy and enthusiasm for future change initiatives.

The model of the pre-implementation phase sets out the work you have just done in the form of a flow chart. By putting together the lists of implications we have derived from our examination of the organisational context and of the innovation itself we can estimate the *adaptive demands* for the change agent group (ie what are our development needs in order to implement this innovation successfully?).

'Significant antecedent conditions' are those things which must be done *before* we can implement the change. The next stage in effecting the change will involve us in planning within an appropriate time scale the sequence of tasks and roles required (network analysis) together with a feedback system for monitoring progress.

Summary

This chapter has introduced some of the key concepts with which we shall be concerned in this work – 'leadership', 'management', 'change agent' and 'organisation'. The organising concepts of the book, 'the organisational context', 'the innovation' and 'the change agent group' were then outlined in the form of a process model for looking at the management of change and development, and a practical exercise was presented to enable the reader to become familiar with the model in use.

All the content areas of the book can be used in conjunction with the model presented in this chapter.

The chapters which follow will focus on each of the three organising concepts in turn. Chapter 2 is concerned with the change agent group, and contains a range of exercises and techniques to help people become more effective as agents of change.

Chapter 3 focuses on the organisational context for change and development. It contains a section on the culture of the school viewed as a configuration of four cultural 'elements', each of which has a part to play according to the challenges or problems which a school may face. This is followed by an instrument for school-based review which provides materials for an assessment of development needs at the whole-school level and a process guide for following up the review phase.

Chapter 4 is concerned with the innovation under consideration. It provides exercises and checklists to help a change agent team to identify and resolve many of the problems and challenges of initiating specific changes in the school context.

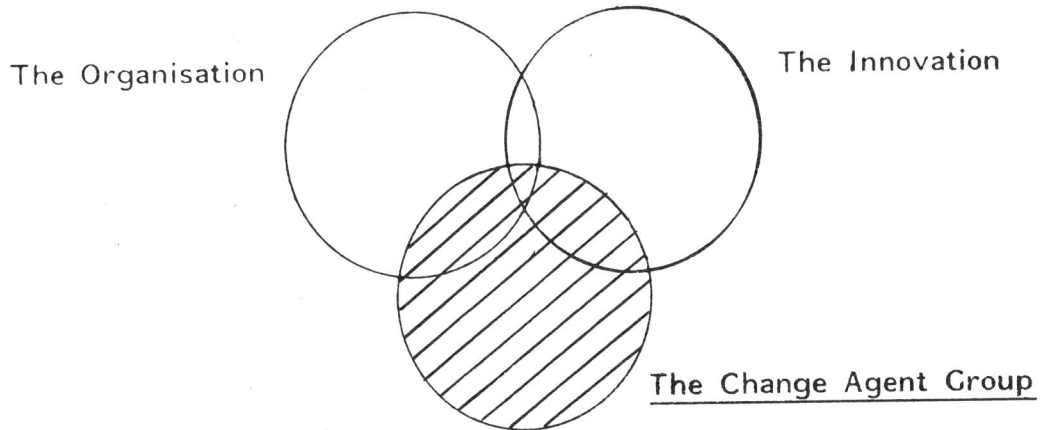

The change agent group

The Organisation

The Innovation

The Change Agent Group

Figure 2.1

This chapter contains a range of exercises which aim to enable the members of a staff team to become more effective agents of change. The exercises focus on individuals, working groups, the role of leadership in an age of change and curriculum dialogue.

The effective change agent
Drawing on our experience

We should like to begin this section with a practical exercise. If you are a member of a change agent team it would be useful to do this as a group exercise, but it can be done on your own if necessary.

Consider a specific change or innovation that you are currently involved in, or have recently undertaken.

What do you think, from your experience, are the key personal qualities, skills and knowledge needed in order to be really effective in managing that change or innovation? (You won't necessarily possess all of these, but it is important to know, ideally, what is required.) We suggest that you spend up to thirty minutes working on this task.

The simplest way of collecting your ideas is by folding a sheet of A4 paper into three equal parts and labelling each part thus:

Qualities
Skills
Knowledge

Note 'Qualities' and 'Skills' will often overlap, so don't worry if the boundary between these becomes blurred as you compile your inventory.

The effective change agent: a conceptual model

We shall now develop a framework to hold together the different requirements of the effective change agent. This 'inventory' is constructed from our own experience of working in schools and colleges together with our knowledge of the literature on the management of change.
The model in its simplest form has four inter-related elements:

– AWARENESS
– COMPETENCE
– WILL
– FEEDBACK

These elements and their relationship to each other are illustrated in Figure 2.2.

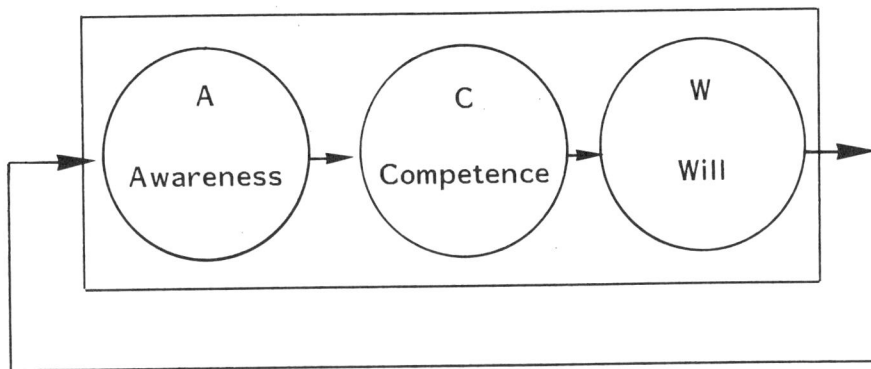

Feedback

Figure 2.2

The rectangle represents the boundary of the self, and the area outside the rectangle the world outside the self. The circle of competence represents the key area of personal qualities and attitudes, skills and knowledge. We have separated two vitally important qualities which play a special part in one's effectiveness – awareness and will. Awareness (of self and of others) ensures accurate perception of a situation and of one's own motivation and feelings. The power of the will, a strangely neglected area in modern psychology, is essential for the completion of tasks, and many intelligent and gifted people fail to achieve their potential due to lack of will.
The final element, feedback, is a pre-requisite for effective change and development. Without information on the results of our actions we cannot learn.
Many of the exercises provided in later sections of this work are designed to help enhance your self-awareness and that of your change agent group members by means of combining self-report inventories like the one you have just completed with mutual feedback. The system recommended for personal feedback is known as 'peer counselling' and will be described in detail at the end of this section.
We shall now present our inventory of the key qualities, skills and knowledge of an effective change agent.

Competence: knowledge, skills and qualities

In this section we shall outline our views on the knowledge, skills and qualities necessary for change agent competence in more detail. The ideas we present can then be incorporated into your own list as an inventory to aid your professional development as a change agent in your school.

KNOWLEDGE
First of all we try to identify those areas of knowledge which are the bases on which change agent competence rests and which will be valid for both internal change agents and external Organisation Development consultants. These knowledge areas can be most readily conceptualised in terms of what we may call 'situational' and 'professional' knowledge.

Situational knowledge will include the mass of basic data which the change agent will need in order to work effectively *in a particular situation*. Thus in a college or school one will need to have basic knowledge of a number of different aspects of the organisation and its environment, for example:

- the 'mission', purposes and policies of the organisation as stated in official policy documents, and as interpreted by those who work there,
- the names, titles, roles, functions and personal characteristics of people who work there,
- the ways in which people, tasks and jobs are related or co-ordinated; the basic rules, regulations, procedures and customs of the school,
- the micro-politics of the school: eg Who are the opinion leaders? Who are the ones who seem to know everything that is going on? Who are the best-liked and most respected members of staff?

- the timetable, working syllabus and curriculum,
- the pastoral or guidance system and its functioning.

This situational knowledge is basic in the sense that it is a foundation for understanding the organisation and the ways people behave there.

Professional knowledge is seen as qualitatively different from situational knowledge in that it normally demands a higher level of conceptual ability and often a considerable time to assimilate the relevant knowledge. It is important too for the change agent or consultant to have a sound experiential base, for theoretical concepts and ideas need to be tested and evaluated against the touchstone of experience and vice versa, so that theory informs practice and practice reforms theory.

A change agent in an educational organisation will need professional knowledge pertaining to a number of areas, for example:

- knowledge of psychology and sociology relevant to human learning and development,
- understanding of organisation theory and group dynamics, including theory of leadership, followership and human motivation,
- knowledge of teaching methods, modes of assessment and evaluation, and the theory of curriculum development and management,
- special curriculum subject knowledge when appropriate, together with appreciation of related subjects or fields,
- knowledge of the considerable literature, theoretical, empirical and prescriptive, that has been written in the field of planned organisational change. The growth of this literature in the past twenty years has been phenomenal, and the biggest problem in monitoring additions to professional knowledge here is the fact that useful research for the change agent can be found in so many diverse disciplines and fields (eg clinical and individual psychology, social psychology, sociology, medicine, management, communication theory, advertising, and social anthropology). The most comprehensive review of the field in its time is the monumental work of Havelock *et al* (1973).

SKILLS

For analytical convenience the skills of the change agent are broken down into three major clusters or groups: updating skills, object-related skills and interpersonal skills. These skills are not discrete in any real sense, as in action the boundaries between them become blurred.

We may picture the relationship between the three groups as seen in Figure 2.3.

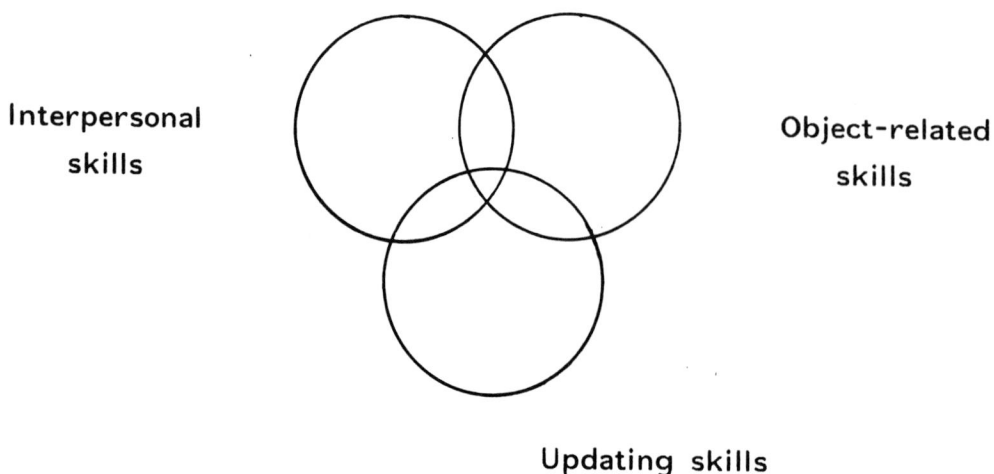

Interpersonal
skills

Object-related
skills

Updating skills

Figure 2.3

Thus a change agent's ability to construct an effective action plan will depend on both a grasp of planning techniques (object-related) and ability to work with the people involved (interpersonal). In the same way, one's ability to keep up to date will depend both on skills in relating to people within the work environment and on the ability to monitor pertinent literature.

Updating skills

This is a very important area concerned with 'topping up' the change agent's fund of professional and situational knowledge so that one is completely up-to-date and well informed: by no means an easy task when the growth of knowledge is so rapid and there are so many sources of valid knowledge.

In this area the change agent must be concerned with issues such as:

- Do I keep abreast of new developments in all the aspects of professional knowledge outlined previously?
- Do I have my finger firmly on the pulse of all those aspects of the school and its environment where I work as change agent or consultant?
- Do I foster and encourage sufficient informal communication with people who can help me keep up to date in both professional and situational terms?

Object-related skills

Under this heading are included the skills of creating, acquiring, modifying and implementing the following:

- instrumentation, diagnostic frameworks and feedback systems for staff development, In-Service training and the diagnosis of individual, group and organisational needs. The change agent should be able to make use of a number of different methods, for example, structured and open-ended interviews, critical incident analysis, and questionnaire-based systems,
- learning experiences with both highly structured and open-ended designs; longer courses, workshops and programmes designed for specific purposes,
- techniques and systems of evaluation.

The human brain has two hemispheres which have differing, specialised functions. Left-hemisphere skills which are relevant to this aspect of change agent competence can be included in this section. These are linear or convergent approaches to problem-solving which we may term 'rational structured thinking', and include such techniques as networking, Critical Path Analysis, Gantt charts, timetabling and scheduling methods, and rational decision-making and planning systems (eg Campbell and Williams, 1982).

More divergent skills and techniques (right hemisphere) useful to the change agent would include Lateral Thinking, Creative Problem Solving, Brainstorming and other deferred judgement methods.

Interpersonal skills

This broad area of interpersonal skills is here subdivided into two categories: task skills and maintenance skills.

Task skills are those relevant to the attainment of goals and would include:

- skills of communicating facts, ideas and feelings to others, listening skills, including the ability to take in both cognitive and affective aspects of communication,
- skills of advocacy: having the abilities to reason out and justify to others an idea or a course of action, and present it with style and vigour,
- ability to lead, inspire and motivate others,
- ability to evaluate and criticise contributions of others in a manner which encourages rather than threatens them,
- ability to accept criticism from others without being over-defensive.

Maintenance skills are those relevant to helping and strengthening others, particularly in the context of a working group. Some of the maintenance skills which are important to a change agent are:

- ability to show warmth and support in interpersonal relationships, especially in relation to encouraging contributions or collaboration from others,
- 'gatekeeping' skills, which involve regulating the flow of communication so that everyone is encouraged to contribute and no one is allowed to dominate in a group,
- process observation and feedback skills: helping others to become aware of the processes and dynamics of groups and consequently learn how to be more effective group members,
- conflict management: skills pertaining to confrontation, mediation and arbitration. Organisations and interpersonal conflict are inextricably linked, and change agents or consultants must possess skills themselves and be able to help others develop skills of confronting conflict, reconciling disagreements and resolving differences.

QUALITIES

This area of qualities, attitudes and values of the change agent is the most important of all for long-term effectiveness. Here we have those factors which will influence skill performance and encourage or inhibit personal development. Although these aspects of the change agent are deeply embedded in the person, nevertheless it is possible to develop new qualities and modify or change existing ones if one is really committed to doing this. We must learn to accept, however, that we cannot hope for instant development in this area but must regard any developmental projects at this level as long-term efforts requiring change in all aspects of ourselves – cognitive, affective and psychomotor.

Task-oriented qualities valuable to the change agent (ie those pertaining to the achievement of goals) are:

- drive (linked with achievement motivation),
- proactivity (being able to look ahead and act to make things happen, rather than simply reacting to outside pressure),
- vision (the ability to see how things might be, and should be),
- helicopter mind (the ability to rise above the trees to see the whole forest, and to descend to work among the trees when appropriate),
- courage (the ability to do what you know is right, even when it may be difficult, painful or unpopular),
- emotional resilience (being able to work well under pressure and developing strategies for managing stress).

Relationship-oriented qualities for the effective change agent (ie those pertaining to getting on well with others) are:

- authenticity (acting with genuineness and honesty in relationships with others),
- empathy (being able to understand the inner world of others, to put yourself in their shoes, and to express your understanding of their perspective),
- positive regard (having a non-judgemental caring for others: a respect for others shown in one's ability to respond to their thoughts, feelings and actions),
- a sense of humour, including the ability to laugh at oneself.

Together with these 'task'- and 'relationship'-oriented qualities we must also stress the importance of trust, in the sense of a basic optimism with regard to other people and to one's self, and above all the need for *self-awareness and a positive self-concept*. In so many ways the change agent's feelings, respect and trust in others appear to depend on this belief and trust in oneself, and we may picture all the most important qualities as both flowing from the self-concept and reinforcing it (see Figure 2.4).

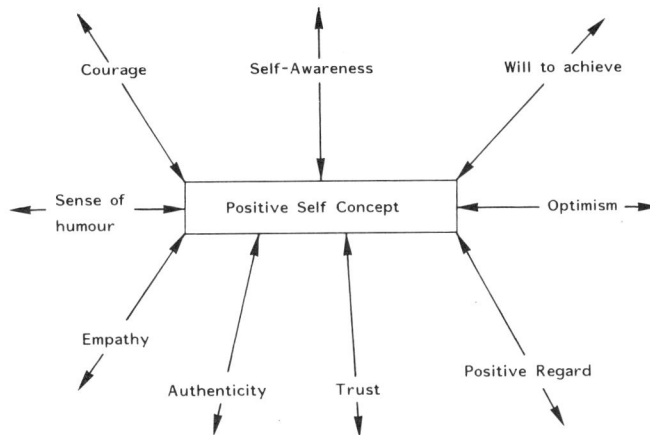

Figure 2.4

Developing our self-awareness

The self-awareness and sensitivity of the change agent will be the most important factor in helping or limiting personal and professional development. Assessment of present knowledge and skills and the learning of new material, skills and techniques will be heavily influenced by one's degree of self-awareness. Without self-awareness we cannot begin to be in charge of our own development:

- we cannot identify key performance areas,
- we cannot analyse our performance, or identify our strengths and weaknesses,
- we cannot set relevant targets or identify concrete objectives,
- we cannot make action plans to help our development,
- we cannot monitor our progress.

Self-knowledge is not only the beginning of wisdom then, but also the beginning of increased personal and professional effectiveness.

We can foster this self-awareness by looking at ourselves and asking questions such as:

- how much time do I spend reflecting about myself?
- how confident am I that I have a reasonable understanding of myself?
- how do I see myself, and how do I feel about myself?
- am I too kind to myself, or too self-critical?
- what are my significant strengths and weaknesses?
- do I really face up to the truth about myself, or do I try to hide the truth about me from myself?

But we can never achieve self-awareness solely by introspection – by gazing and reflecting upon our thoughts, perceptions, emotions, motives and actions. Introspection will provide us with understanding of our experience, but a complete self-awareness requires knowledge of our behaviour too. For this we need the help of others: it takes two to know one fully.

Self-awareness through feedback

I am aware of my experience (inner processes) but I cannot see my behaviour (outer processes). My colleagues can see my behaviour, but cannot see my experience. I can see my colleagues' behaviour, but not their inner experience.
My colleagues are aware of their experience, but cannot see their own behaviour.
For a complete self-awareness, then, we need to augment the knowledge gained by introspection with the knowledge obtained by feedback from others about our behaviour.

Self-review exercise

The objectives of this exercise are:

- to review our strengths and self-chosen development challenge,
- to help each other through the processes of decision-making and action-planning.

Step 1

Look through the list of qualities, skills and knowledge you have made, together with those from our list which may be appropriate to your work. Award yourself a 'star' mark by the side of each one which you believe is one of your strengths.

Step 2

Now look through those items which you did not star and identify a *development challenge.*

A development challenge is some aspect of our expertise which is important to our effectiveness as an agent of change and which we should like to improve. It may be a personal quality, a skill, an area of knowledge, or some combination of these.

Step 3

Write a brief memorandum about your development challenge. This should include notes on:

- what *exactly* is your challenge?
- in what sort of situations will you feel more effective when you have improved this area of your expertise?
- how will you recognise that you are improving? What will be the signs or indicators?

Step 4

Be prepared to talk through your development challenge with a colleague, using the method of *peer counselling* which is explained in the pages following.

Self-awareness through peer counselling

Peer counselling is a self-directed method of personal development which involves the use of the small group in learning (3–4 persons) but affirms the autonomy and importance of the individual. The process is in many respects similar to Rogerian counselling but differs in its emphasis on the use of colleagues in the small counselling group, and in its establishment of a firm structure for the collection of data and the 'ground rules' of the counselling interview.

It must be emphasised here that counselling is viewed as a developmental, educational process and not merely a therapeutic exercise.

It is felt that the firm structure provided by the 'technology' for personal data gathering and counselling interview provides an organised format in which people can feel secure while they are learning the requisite skills. It is envisaged that, with practice, members of a peer counselling group will modify the structure to suit their own needs as they become more confident and competent within the counselling process.

Using peer counselling as a tool for development and change

This section outlines the process of peer counselling. It is a structured method of practising the helping process with colleagues and can be used in conjunction with many of the exercises in this manual. The exercises simply provide a topic area for the change agent to focus on, such as 'effectiveness' or 'leadership' and peer counselling becomes the vehicle by means of which decisions and plans are made and action follows.

Staff should be encouraged, but never coerced to use this method, and it is important that everyone participating in peer counselling acknowledges that everything covered in the interview and feedback session is confidential to the group unless exceptions are agreed by all concerned. When peer counselling is well established in a school it can result in better teamwork, reduction of stress levels and raising of staff morale in addition to more effective professional development for individuals. But to achieve the best results it should be built into the school's INSET structure once it has had a successful trial.

The method of peer counselling

One way of facilitating professional development after working through the Change Agent Effectiveness Framework is by means of a peer counselling development group. This is ideally a small group of three or four colleagues who share the following characteristics:

 - a basic liking and respect for each other,
 - a common desire to develop professional knowledge and skills,
 - an appreciation of the need for help and support from others in striving for professional development.

Members of a peer counselling group subscribe not only to the need for others to help in their personal and professional development, but also to the need for a self-directed method which affirms the autonomy and importance of the individual. The different personal data collection systems in this guide then become a map of territory to explore in the early stages of a change or development project.

Let us take an example of three colleagues who agree to undertake a professional development project together. They allocate some periods of time to the project, and decide on a suitable place to meet, which may be at work or at their homes. It is important, however, no matter where they meet, that they should have the privacy and freedom from interruption needed to practise peer counselling. They decide to use the Change Agent Effectiveness Framework and agree a commitment by each person to go through peer counselling interviews with successive phases of:

 - diagnosis (Where am I now in relation to my development challenge?)
 - decision-making (Where do I wish to be? How feasible is this?)
 - planning (What, then, am I going to do? How shall I do it?)
 - evaluation (What is happening to my plan? How am I progressing?)

The basic vehicle for these four phases of diagnosis, decision-making, planning and evaluation is the peer counselling group. The three colleagues initiate this by agreeing functions within the group as follows:

The client: this is the person whose professional development is under consideration. After a period of data collection, based on the Change Agent Effectiveness Framework, the client will discuss his or her personal diagnosis and analysis of needs. The data collection phase is carried out thoroughly by the client so that the diagnostic phase of the counselling interview can draw on empirical fact as much as possible.

The counsellor: this is the person whose primary task is that of 'friendly critic', helping the client to conduct a self-appraisal, to decide on the action he or she wishes to take, to make action plans, and to assess progress.

The effective counsellor will be one who is genuine in the relationship: she will show that she accepts and values her colleague as a person by demonstrating an unconditional, non-judgemental caring, and able to demonstrate understanding of the meaning of the peer counselling process for her colleague.

The interview should not be an interrogation, therefore, but a test of the counsellor's interpersonal skills: of ability to relate and empathise, while exercising analytical skills.

In my experience, teachers, perhaps because of their training and socialisation, appear more prone than others to see the world in terms of judgemental or evaluative constructs. They may also tend to see their role primarily in an 'expert' mode, as solvers of other people's problems. For teachers accustomed to operating in a didactic, as opposed to a facilitative mode, a conscious effort of will may be necessary to help the mind to 'unfreeze' sufficiently to suspend judgement. The prime goal in peer counselling is not to judge or evaluate a colleague, but to help the client, sympathetically but firmly, to appraise herself and to make her own judgements and decisions. The effective counsellor will ask questions which help a colleague to focus on the *basis* for her judgements – questions such as:

- What causes you to say this?
- How do you know this is so?
- What evidence would you cite to support this?

A useful rule of thumb for the counsellor is–if the ratio of talk between client and counsellor is less than three to one in the client's favour (ie 75% to 25%) she is almost certainly doing too much talking and not enough listening.

The observer: the task of the person in this role is to remain silent, and as inconspicuous as possible throughout the interview. The observer should focus attention on both the content and process of the interview, making brief notes on her observations so that she can give a more objective view of the counselling interview as feedback to both client and counsellor. The observer should note behaviour of either person in the interview which particularly helped or hindered the process of diagnosis or decision-making, or the relationship between the two parties. (See Figure 2.5 for a format for recording these aspects of the interview.) At the end of the peer counselling interview, the observer initiates a discussion with her colleagues based on these observations.

When presenting feedback on the interview it is suggested that observers talk about the positive 'helpful' sections first. In talking about the 'hindering' aspects it helps if one emphasises *future* behaviour rather than focusing too much on things past (eg 'I think you would be more helpful to your client if you slowed down the pace of the interview and created some pauses to give space to your client', instead of 'I felt you hurried and pressurised your client').

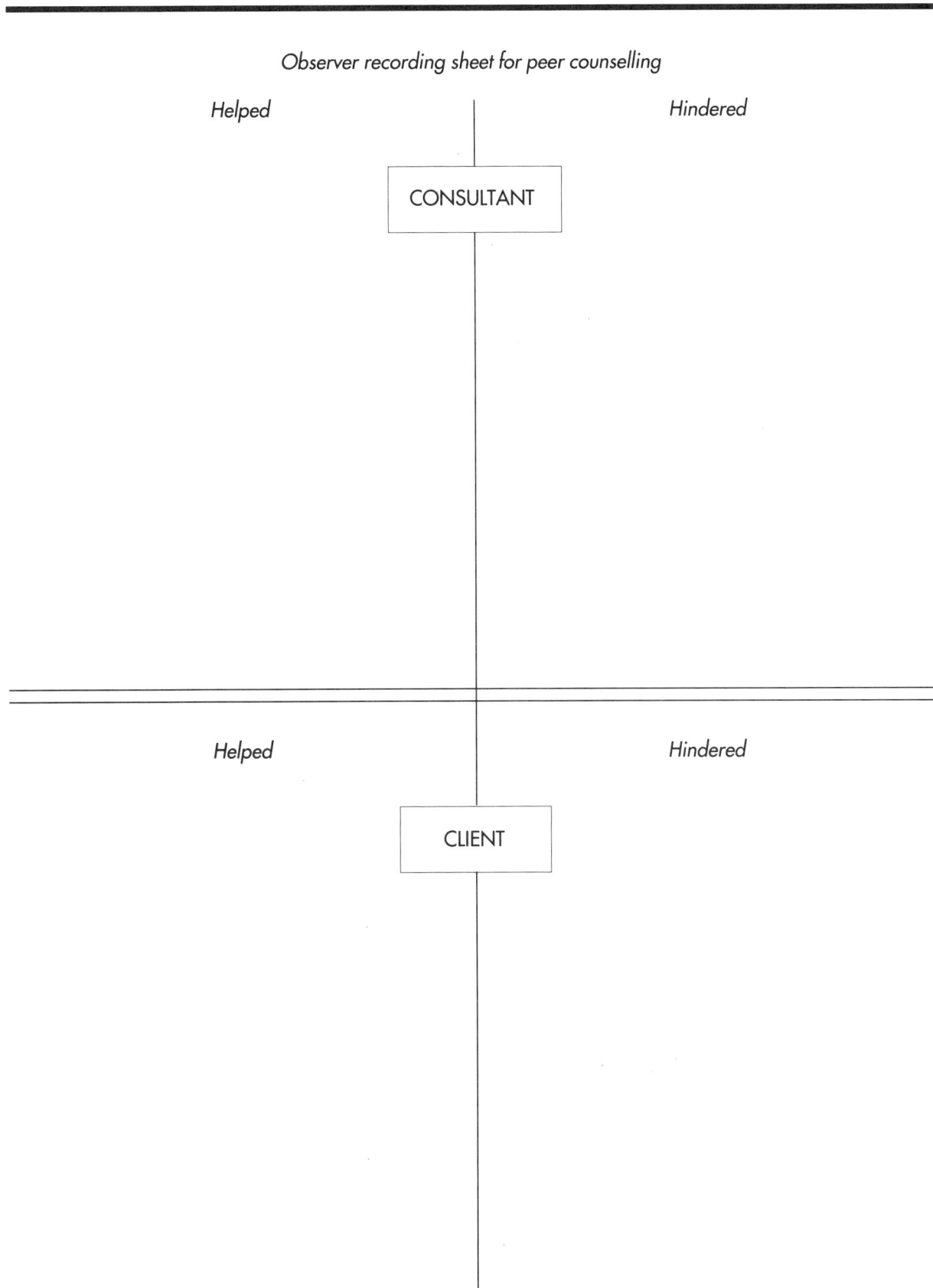

Observer recording sheet for peer counselling

Helped   *Hindered*

CONSULTANT

Helped   *Hindered*

CLIENT

Figure 2.5

The peer counselling interview gives one the opportunity to practise three groups of skills of great relevance to both effective consultation, and to personal and professional development in the widest sense (see Figure 2.6).

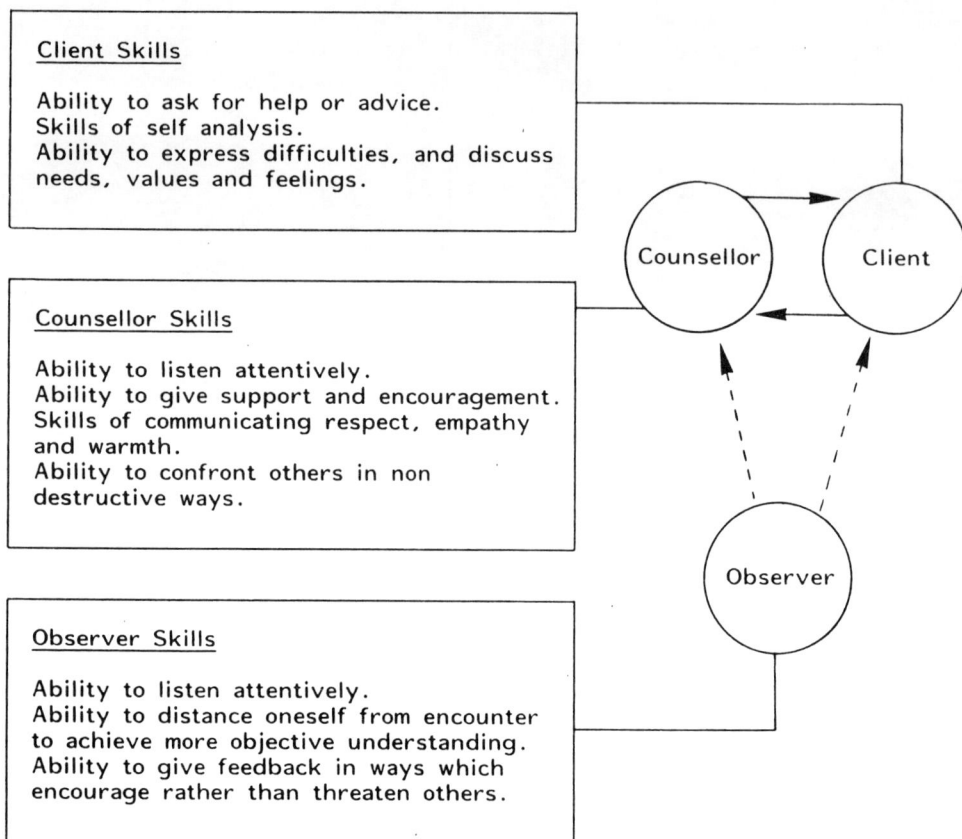

Client Skills

Ability to ask for help or advice.
Skills of self analysis.
Ability to express difficulties, and discuss needs, values and feelings.

Counsellor Skills

Ability to listen attentively.
Ability to give support and encouragement.
Skills of communicating respect, empathy and warmth.
Ability to confront others in non destructive ways.

Observer Skills

Ability to listen attentively.
Ability to distance oneself from encounter to achieve more objective understanding.
Ability to give feedback in ways which encourage rather than threaten others.

Figure 2.6

The three colleagues who form the peer counselling development group agree to change roles the next time they meet, and on subsequent occasions, so that each of them in turn will have the opportunity to be client, counsellor and observer.

Over time they each pass through phases of a development cycle which may be pictured as in Figure 2.7.

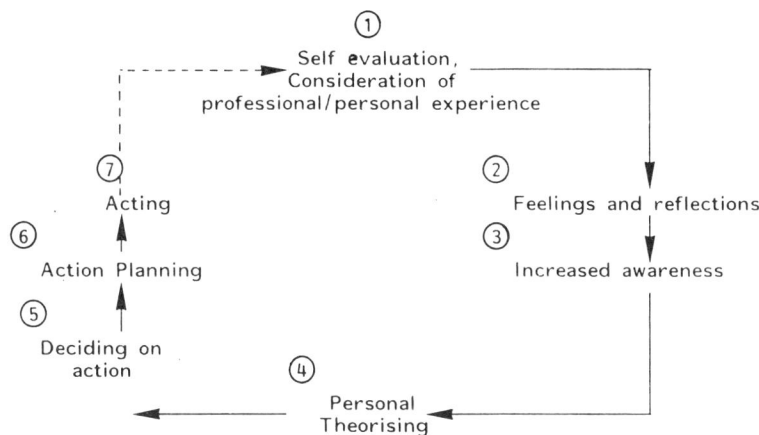

Figure 2.7

In this cycle the client's development process begins with the decision to conduct a self-evaluation, and the first peer counselling session(s) are covered by stages 1 to 4: going through a counselling interview to identify needs or problems, sharing feelings about the needs, and building a personal 'theory' about what is required as a result of this increased awareness.

The second half of the development cycle, stages 5 to 7, is concerned with the making of decisions and action plans based on personal theorising and with the implementation of those plans.

The cycle is completed and re-initiated when the action phase provides the individual with feedback about progress and raises the issue of a continuing self-evaluation of professional experience and practice.

Change agents in management positions who wish to continue their professional development within a broader framework which goes beyond the model used here may wish to consider using a resource with a managerial focus: *Improving your Professional Effectiveness: a Handbook for Managers in Education* (Elliott-Kemp and Williams, 1981). This is a comprehensive inventory and question bank incorporating questions on a wide range of development areas such as knowledge of policies, plans and resources, professional skills (including communication and decision-making skills) and personal qualities relevant to professional effectiveness for the headteacher, principal, deputy head or head of department.

Further examples of the peer counselling method used in conjunction with other evaluative frameworks can be found in Elliott-Kemp (1981), Elliott-Kemp and Williams (1981) and Elliott-Kemp and Rogers (1982).

References

CAMPBELL, J. H. and WILLIAMS, G. L. (1982) *Decision Making in Education Management: the Technique of Issue Analysis*, PAVIC Publications, Sheffield City Polytechnic, UK.

ELLIOTT-KEMP, J. (1981) *Staff Development in Schools: a Framework for Diagnosis of Individual Teacher Development Needs*, PAVIC Publications, Sheffield City Polytechnic, UK.

ELLIOTT-KEMP, J. and WILLIAMS, G. L. (1981) *Improving Your Professional Effectiveness: a Handbook for Managers in Education*, PAVIC Publications, Sheffield City Polytechnic, UK.

ELLIOTT-KEMP, J. and ROGERS, C. (1982) *The Effective Teacher: a Person-Centred Development Guide*, PAVIC Publications, Sheffield City Polytechnic, UK.

HAVELOCK, R.G. *et al* (1973) *Planning for Innovation through Dissemination and Utilisation of Knowledge*, Centre for Research on Utilisation of Scientific Knowledge, Michigan University.

The Behavioural Profile

The exercise which follows is designed to help you improve your self-awareness and your awareness of your colleagues.

IMPORTANT

It is essential to *do* the exercise before you read about it.

Do not be tempted to dip into the interpretation section until you have completed your profile diagram.

THE BEHAVIOURAL PROFILE

The purposes of this instrument are:
- to help you achieve a deeper understanding of some aspects of your own interpersonal style,
- to identify development challenges related to the work situation,
- to give you a framework for appreciating some of the ways in which people may find difficulty in working together as a team.

Instructions

Please respond to the sixteen statements in the Behavioural Profile on page 27 to give the most truthful picture of you as you see yourself. Ask yourself with each statement 'To what extent does this describe me?' Then use the Response Sheet to record your responses, placing a circle around the number in the appropriate box as follows:

2	1	1	2
This is not at all true of me	I don't think this really describes me	This describes me to some extent	This is very true of me

BEHAVIOURAL PROFILE: SELF-REPORT STATEMENTS

1. I prefer involvement in change to keeping things running on as they are.
2. I can usually keep things in perspective, so that I seldom over-inflate the importance of any problem.
3. I get more satisfaction from working on a task on my own than as a member of a group.
4. I don't tolerate fools gladly.
5. I am more comfortable when I can maintain a proper social distance and avoid getting too deeply involved with my colleagues.
6. Much of the success I have achieved in my life is due to my ability to think and act more quickly than other people.
7. I sometimes find it difficult to 'switch off' and relax after a hectic day.
8. I am more comfortable in a helping or counselling role with my colleagues rather than one involving analysis and critical evaluation of their work.
9. I know my own limitations and consequently seldom take on tasks or projects beyond my capabilities.
10. I attach equal importance to strength of feeling and passionate sincerity in my colleagues as I do to disciplined thought and impartial judgement.
11. I tend to feel impatient with people who think or act more slowly than I.
12. I am good at showing enthusiasm and appreciation for the ideas and achievements of my colleagues.
13. I am usually quick to seize any opportunity which arises.
14. I can usually remain calm and unruffled, even though others are showing signs of panic.
15. I would tend to describe myself as more of a pessimist than an optimist.
16. I'm happier fighting for my own ideas than working towards a compromise with others.

BEHAVIOURAL PROFILE: RESPONSE SHEET

Disagree				Agree		
1	E	2	1	1	2	R	1
2	D	2	1	1	2	O	2
3	R	2	1	1	2	E	3
4	R	2	1	1	2	E	4
5	R	2	1	1	2	E	5
6	O	2	1	1	2	D	6
7	O	2	1	1	2	D	7
8	E	2	1	1	2	R	8
9	D	2	1	1	2	O	9
10	E	2	1	1	2	R	10
11	O	2	1	1	2	D	11
12	E	2	1	1	2	R	12
13	O	2	1	1	2	D	13
14	D	2	1	1	2	O	14
15	R	2	1	1	2	E	15
16	O	2	1	1	2	D	16

Constructing your Behavioural Profile

To complete your profile diagram you will first need to total your scores in each of the four areas covered in the framework.

The scoring key for your profile can be found at the extreme left and right sides of the response sheet in the form of a column of letters (R, O, E, D etc) on each side.

You will need to transfer the scores you have ringed, ① or ②, to the appropriate space in the table below. Begin with your scores on the left side of the sheet, working from the top to the bottom of the sheet; then enter your scores from the right side of the sheet.

	Left side	Right side	Total
R	+		
O	+		
E	+		
D	+		

Now calculate your total score for each of the profile areas 'R', 'O', 'E' and 'D' by adding together your left-and right-side scores for each letter, entering each score total in the right-hand column of the table.

Your score for each letter should now be transferred to the blank Behavioural Profile form on page 30 by entering a mark at the appropriate place on each of the four polarities, 'R', 'O', 'E' and 'D'.

BEHAVIOURAL PROFILE FORM

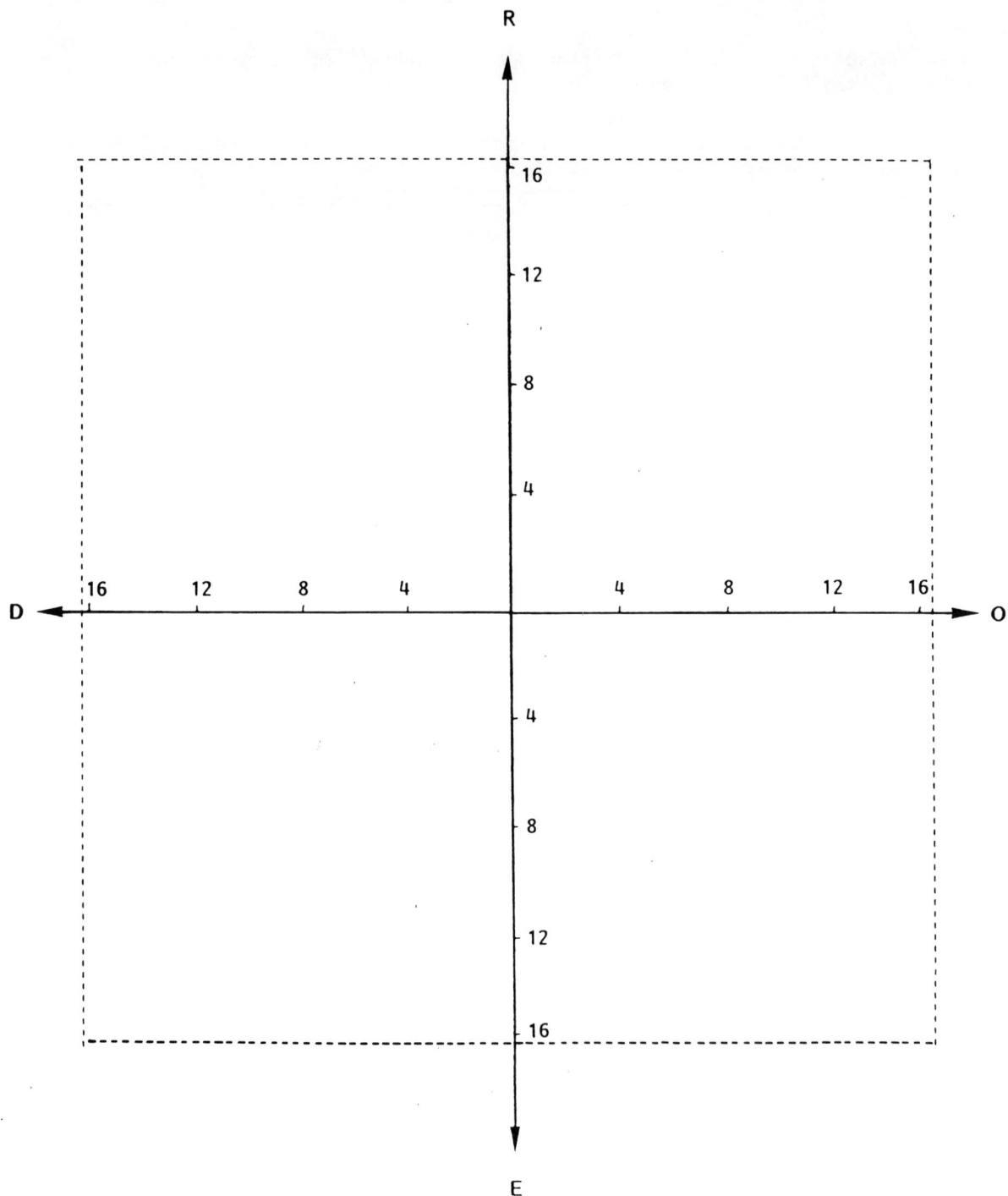

```
                                    R
                                    ↑
        ┌ ─ ─ ─ ─ ─ ─ ─ ─ ─ ─ ─ ─ ─ ─ ─ ─ ─ ─ ─ ─ ─ ─ ┐
        |                         ├ 16                  |
        |                         |                     |
        |                         ├ 12                  |
        |                         |                     |
        |                         ├ 8                   |
        |                         |                     |
        |                         ├ 4                   |
        |                         |                     |
     ┌16      12      8       4    |    4      8      12    16┐
   D ←─┼──────┼───────┼───────┼────┼────┼──────┼──────┼────┼──→ O
        |                         |                     |
        |                         ├ 4                   |
        |                         |                     |
        |                         ├ 8                   |
        |                         |                     |
        |                         ├ 12                  |
        |                         |                     |
        |                         ├ 16                  |
        └ ─ ─ ─ ─ ─ ─ ─ ─ ─ ─ ─ ─ ─ ─ ─ ─ ─ ─ ─ ─ ─ ─ ┘
                                    ↓
                                    E
```

© John Elliott-Kemp
Helios International

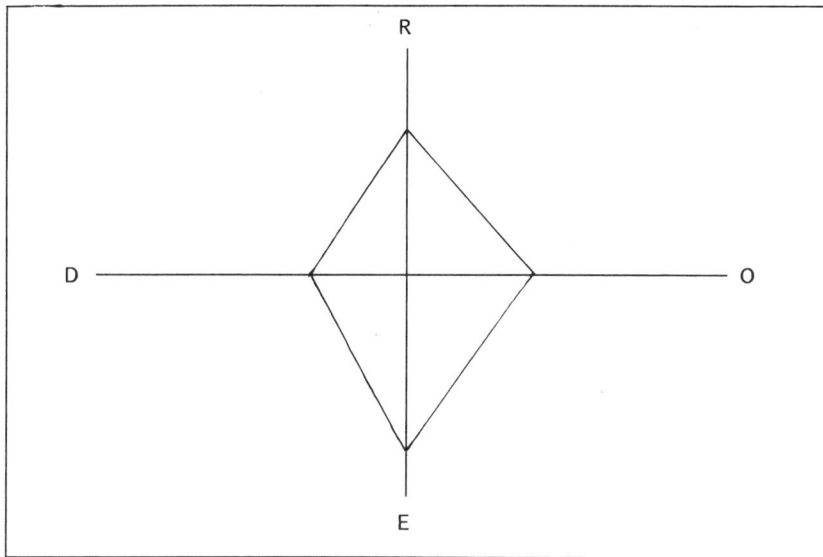

Figure 2.8

Your profile is completed by drawing straight lines to connect your 'R' and 'O' score points, 'O' and 'E' points, 'E' and 'D', and finally 'D' and 'R'.

You are now in a position to interpret your profile.

NOTE TO FACILITATOR OR TRAINER

The section on interpretation of the profile can be presented in the form of a lecture, or copies of the following pages can be given to participants who work in small groups (3-4 people) to discuss their profiles, how they feel about their own profile, and how they perceive each other in terms of the different dimensions of the profile.

INTERPRETING THE BEHAVIOURAL PROFILE

It is suggested that you regard your profile as a mirror which is reflecting a particular picture of you. Mirrors can provide accurate reflections, or they may be distorted in some way. Your profile diagram has no validity in the scientific sense, but the framework used is based on conceptual models supported by many different sources in psychology, management and organisation theory. Reference sources and theoretical background are provided at the end of this section on the Behavioural Profile.

The initial challenge of this exercise is to use the profile 'mirror' as a first step in gaining increased self-awarenes, firstly by introspection and reflection:

– Do I see myself in accordance with my profile?

– How do I see myself as differing from my profile?

– What evidence do I have?

Secondly, I can ask for feedback from those who know me well:

– 'How do you, my colleague or friend, see me in terms of the different dimensions of the profile?'

– 'Why do you see me like this?'

Increased awareness, however, is just the first stage. The next challenge is to identify some aspect of ourselves which we would like to improve – our *development challenge* chosen from some aspects of the profile. We then use our close colleagues as resources or advisers to help us achieve our goal, or at least improve ourselves in the area of our development challenge.

Interpretation of the Behavioural Profile

The framework which follows reflects some of the most important aspects of a person. It encompasses a person's

- – perceptual bias,
- – prevailing state and mental set,
- – dominant social motivation,
- – competing value dimensions pertinent to the evaluation of social action.

The vertical polarity

The model is built around two intersecting axes or polarities. The vertical axis reflects structure in both degree and kind. The bottom end of this polarity emphasises clear or tight structure, objectivity and certainty, while the top emphasises loose structure, subjectivity and uncertainty (see Figure 2.9).

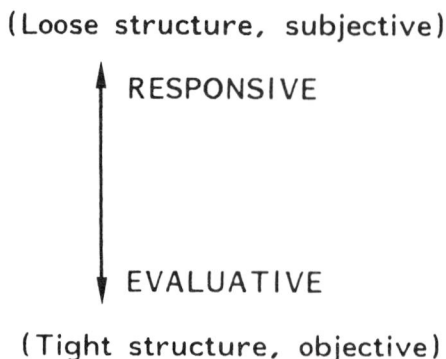

(Loose structure, subjective)

↑ RESPONSIVE

↓ EVALUATIVE

(Tight structure, objective)

Figure 2.9

Storr (1988) cites Worringer's distinction between 'Abstraction' and 'Empathy' (the subject of a chapter in Jung's *Psychological Types* (1971)) as essentially reflecting this polarity. Worringer asserts man's 'urge to empathy' and 'urge to abstraction' as the major dimensions of modern aesthetics. The urge to empathy finds its gratification in the beauty of the living, organic world, whereas the urge to abstraction finds its beauty in the crystalline, the inorganic or in abstract laws.

These fundamental differences between adults have also been identified among young children. Gardner (1980), distinguishes two broad types of children, whom he terms 'patterners' and 'dramatists'. 'Patterners' can be recognised by their fascination with the physical attributes of objects, their form, size, colour and shape. They tend to be more interested in the world of patterns, regularities and configurations than in social relationships. 'Dramatists', on the other hand, show a strong preference for events, processes and actions involving living creatures. Patterners can be readily identified by their preference for drawing, building or making regular arrays or numerical patterns. The dramatists, in contrast, are more likely to engage in make-believe play, story-telling and social encounter.

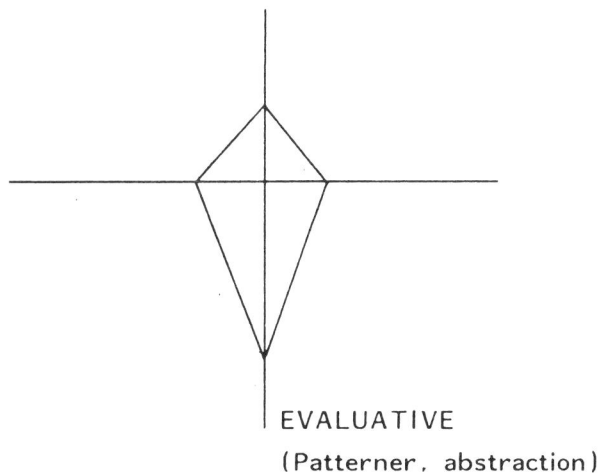

EVALUATIVE
(Patterner, abstraction)
Figure 2.10

A profile which is strongly biased towards the 'evaluative' polarity will tend to indicate a person who

- is interested in ideas and abstractions, and the orderly presentation of facts and ideas,
- values logic and rigour,
- is capable of offering negative evaluation or criticism but may not always possess the social skills to present it in a sensitive manner,
- may be very effective working alone but not always comfortable as a member of a team,
- may be intolerant of others who are different, uncomfortable with situations or ideas of high uncertainty or ambiguity, and suspicious or fearful of the intuitive or non-rational.

A group of high 'evaluatives' together may produce excellent critiques of each other's ideas, but, because of their fascination with 'truth' and 'objectivity' may produce more talk than action. High evaluatives are far more likely to feel threatened by an exercise such as this one than those with different configurations. They are also much more likely to reject the validity of their profile and may need sensitive feedback from colleagues on what they are 'really' like (objective truth).

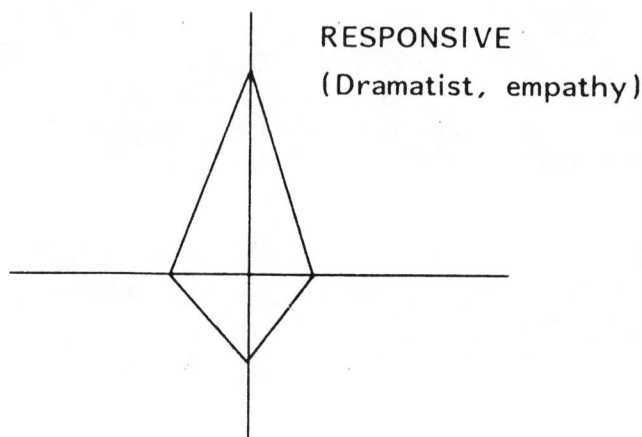

RESPONSIVE
(Dramatist, empathy)

Figure 2.11

In contrast, high 'responsive' profiles tend to be held by people who

- are gregarious and highly sociable,
- like variety, excitement and change,
- are considerate and supportive colleagues,
- value relationships with others above abstract considerations like 'truth' or 'beauty',
- emphasise the helping relationship as one of the most important and rewarding aspects of their work, rather than 'knowledge' or 'subjects' which tend to be more favoured by high 'evaluators',
- have affiliation motivation as their dominant social motive (the need to be accepted, needed, liked by others).

High responsives make good colleagues to have around one in a school. Some of their dysfunctional aspects, however, can be the tendency of a 'responsive' group to be cosy and uncritical and for individual high affiliators to make themselves ineffective in their own work because they can never say 'no' to a colleague's request for help or advice. Such people are often exploited by their colleagues because of their unselfish willingness to help another, but often do not realise that they are allowing their affiliation motive to rule their lives, instead of channelling it to suit their purposes. This is known as the 'Helpful Harry' (or Harriet) syndrome.

The horizontal polarity

Dynamic   ⟷   Oceanic
(External focus)   (Internal focus)

Figure 2.12

The two extremes of this polarity reflect the direction of a person's attention and energy in relation to change and development. The high 'Oceanic' has an internal focus and consequently emphasises inner development, a calm contemplative approach and, in extreme cases, a tendency to withdraw from the outer world. The 'Dynamic' person, on the other hand, has an external focus concerned with active engagement with the outer world, exploration and acquisition. In addition to their differing internal or external focus these two extremes tend to have very different life styles, rhythms and approaches to time.

The horizontal polarity also represents the autonomic nervous system or ANS, deeply embedded in all human kind and underpinning the survival and development of the species. The autonomic nervous system comprises two sub-systems called the sympathetic and parasympathetic systems.

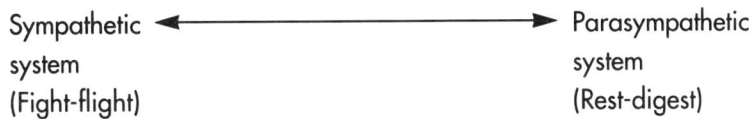

Sympathetic ←——————————————→ Parasympathetic
system   system
(Fight-flight)   (Rest-digest)

Figure 2.13

The parasympathetic system is responsible for the human 'steady-state' or homeostasis, a state in which we use long, slow breathing movements and alpha waves in the brain produce a relaxed, contemplative mood. It is this 'oceanic' aspect of our nature which helps us rest and digest and which is also the basis of our ability to 'switch off' after a hectic or stressful day. The parasympathetic or oceanic domain is also the source of our spiritual life.

Whenever we perceive danger or threat the sympathetic (dynamic) side of our nature is alerted. This results in an immediate state of readiness for flight or fight due to massive amounts of adrenalin and cholesterol flooding through our system. The heart beats more quickly and both breathing rhythm and brain waves change from long, slow oceanic patterns to rapid, shallow movements. When the sympathetic system is alerted we immediately become tense and ready for action; indeed this side of our nature has played a major role in our survival as a species. However, the dangers which triggered off the sympathetic nervous system in the days of the cave men and women usually provided the means for using up the adrenalin and cholesterol accumulating in the system either through fight or through flight. Modern man or woman, however, has fewer acceptable outlets for immediate physical action when the sympathetic system is triggered, especially in the work environment. Consequently the surplus adrenalin and cholesterol linger on in the body as poisons.

People with high 'dynamic' profiles will tend to have a low sympathetic system threshold. They are undoubtedly people who make things happen and cause waves wherever they go, but their long-term effectiveness may be suspect unless they learn to prioritise and manage their energy appropriately. The high dynamic syndrome of 'A-type' behaviour is extremely well documented (Friedman and Rosenman, 1974; Friedman and Ulmer, 1984) and the numerous accounts of resulting ulcers, coronaries, breakdown and burnout make depressing reading. The 'A-type' dynamic is very difficult to help: since this condition is linked to power motivation (the need to control people and situations, the need to compete and win at virtually anything, no matter how trivial) it involves changing the way one perceives the world. Even when one has developed strategies and tactics for coping with ultra high power motivation it will still be there within the person, like a bubbling spring waiting to emerge whenever a situation with 'power potential' arises. The management of human potential and stress and burnout proofing, especially with reference to A-type behaviour, are featured in Elliott-Kemp (1986) which explores different types of stress and the 'dark potential' of each of the extremes of the polarities in the behavioural profile.

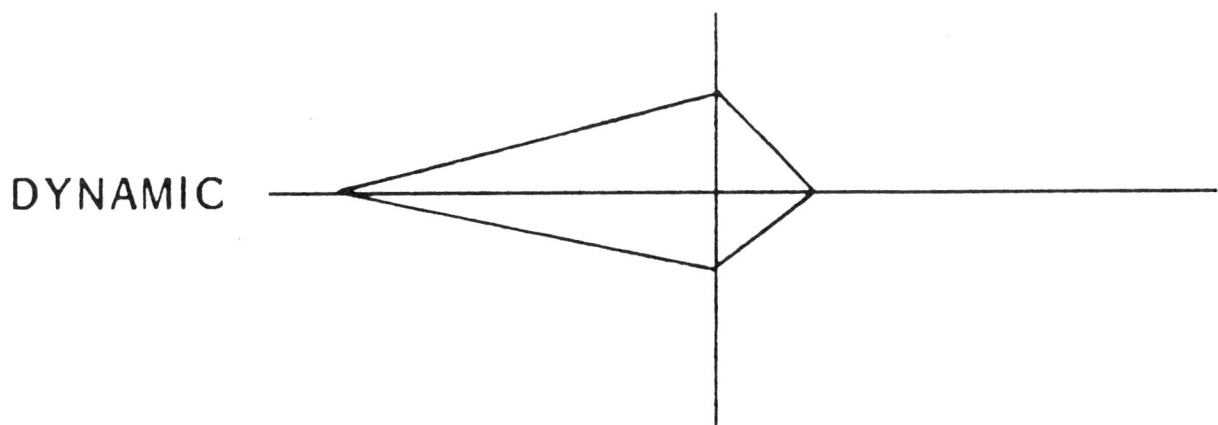

DYNAMIC

Figure 2.14

A profile which is strongly biased towards the 'dynamic' polarity will tend to indicate a person who

- is dominant and action-oriented in work relationships,
- enjoys taking risks and cutting corners,
- thrives on competition,
- is decisive and quick to judge,
- seems to have abundant energy for a challenge,
- has an outgoing nature,
- may be highly calculative in relationships and something of a politician,
- may lack a sense of priorities and consequently squander a lot of time and energy,
- may be lacking in self-awareness,
- may try to run life's marathon like a sprint,
- may, like the hare in the fable, be scornful of those perceived as tortoises.

In the world of big business and industry the 'Dynamics' seem to be typified by the dashing young executives of the so-called 'enterprise society'. Those who reach the very top, however, and learn to stay there, seem more often to have developed their Oceanic side and employ the 'Dynamics' to do all the running about for them. Management is essentially getting things done with and through other people: the big danger with many 'A-type' Dynamics is that they may try to do everything themselves.

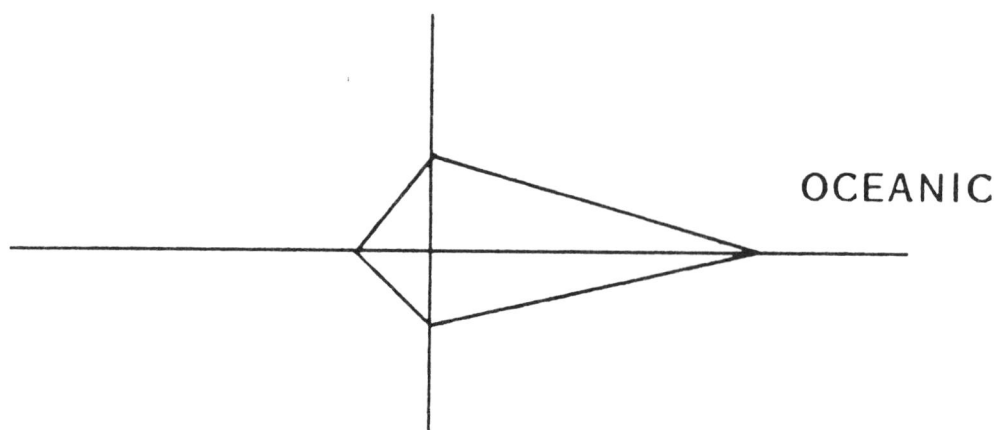

Figure 2.15

'Oceanic' profiles tend to be held by people who

- reflect before judging or acting,
- are calm, balanced, and not easily ruffled,
- have a keen sense of proportion and priorities,
- because of their reflective nature are high in self-awareness,
- tend to take a long-term perspective, in contrast to the typical pragmatism of the 'Dynamic' person,
- may be perceived as too easy-going or indecisive by others (especially by Dynamics).

These inner-outer distinctions between the Oceanic and the Dynamic are at the heart of the difference between traditional Eastern and Western philosophy (Taggart and Robey, 1981; Quinn, 1984). The typical Western view emphasises the imposition of order on the world of nature and the manipulation of people and things to attain goals (Dynamic). The Eastern view, in contrast, emphasises the oneness of nature and the connectedness of all things. It tends to be associated with the acceptance of things as they are and the avoidance of unnecessary action (Oceanic).

Leadership and the Behavioural Profile

The literature on leadership emphasises three major factors or variables in chosing a style which is most appropriate:

- concern for the task or goal to be achieved,
- concern for people and their needs and feelings, including the needs of the working group,
- the unique nature of the situation.

It is the third of these factors, the situation, which should influence the degree to which concern for the task or concern for people should take priority.

But people tend to have a 'natural' style, the one with which they are most comfortable and where they are probably most skilled and confident. There will be occasions when this intuitive style will be most effective; equally, there will be occasions when it will be inappropriate. Effective leadership, in the long term, will depend on a person's situational judgement and on the ability to switch from task-centred to people-centred behaviour, or vice-versa, or to behave in ways which embody an appropriate mix of the two. Task-centred leadership is particularly relevant for short-term goals, including crisis management, whereas people-centred leadership is more relevant to long-term issues such as team spirit, staff morale and the building of trust.

A person's natural or intuitive leadership style is usually reflected in their Behavioural Profile. The two scores which are most relevant here are the Dynamic (task-centred) and Responsive (people-centred), and a comparison of these scores in a person's profile provides the indicator of natural leadership style. The same style will tend to be reflected in working with adult colleagues or with children, ie teaching style.

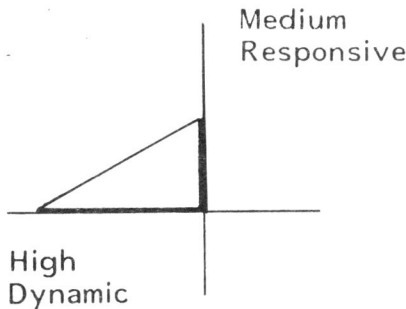

Medium Responsive

High Dynamic

Figure 2.16

This is the profile of a task-centred leader. This person is not without concern for people but that is not her prime concern. She puts achievement of results first.

The more the profile is skewed towards the Dynamic side, and the lower the Responsive score, the more the leader will tend to be achievement-oriented and the tighter will be the monitoring and control of people's work. The ultimate task-centred leader (maximum Dynamic score and little or no score on the Responsive axis) is the 'slave-driver'.

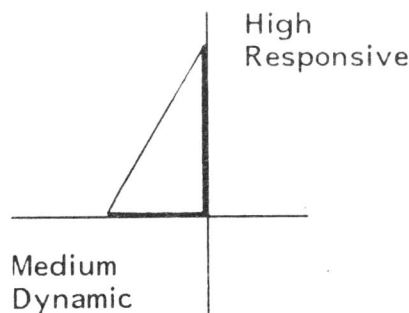

High Responsive

Medium Dynamic

Figure 2.17

This is the profile of a people-centred leader. She believes in the importance of results but feels that in order to get things done people need to feel secure in their work, knowing their leader always has their well-being in mind and will look after their interests. This is her prime goal. She differs from the Dynamic leader in that her style is not so much *directive*, working on people, as *facilitative*, working alongside or among people.

The more the profile is skewed towards the Responsive polarity, with a corresponding decrease in the dynamic score, the nearer the leadership style approaches that of the final example of leadership in the works of the classical Chinese poet Lao Tse:

With this type of leader,
When the sun has set
And all the tasks completed,
The people say
'We did it ourselves'.

The ultimate Responsive leader is uncomfortable with the title of formal leader, avoids the limelight and attention which other leaders seek and aspires in the end to be 'one of the gang' – in a formal sense, the invisible leader.

The four triangles of the profile

The size of the triangles in a profile (measured in area) is likely to be significant in the same way as the length of a polarity score line: a large triangle or high score line will indicate a strength and a small triangle or low score line will tend to indicate a development challenge.

We shall begin with the bottom left and top right-hand triangles:

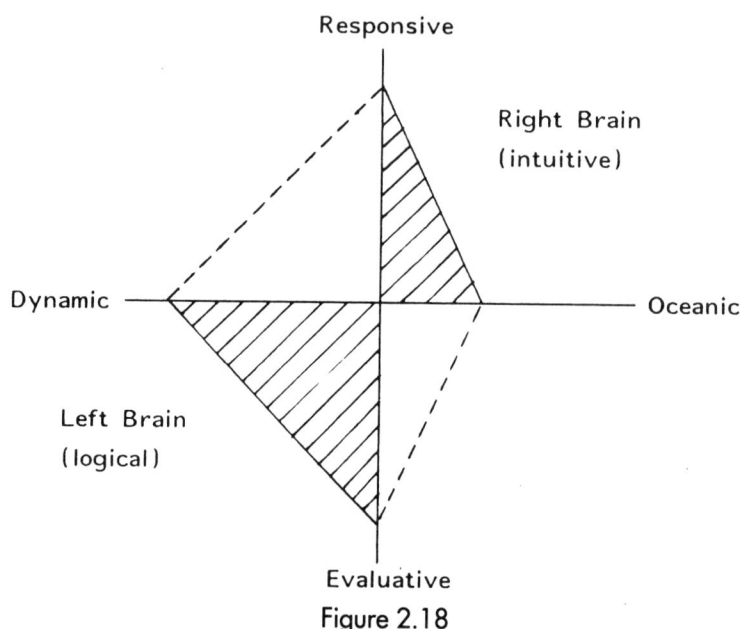

Figure 2.18

These two triangles reflect the two hemispheres of the human brain which function in very distinctive ways and are co-ordinated by a complex bundle of fibres called the corpus callosum. The left hemisphere relies on logical, analytical thinking which is timebound and sequential (step by step) in its way of operating. The right hemisphere tends to function in a completely different way. It proceeds by intuitive, imaginative leaps, is time-free and spontaneous – thinking in terms of 'wholes' rather than 'parts'.

Both hemispheres have a part to play in human creativity and problem-solving: the right hemisphere, with its linkage to that great well of fantasy and ideas, the subconscious, provides the initial breakthrough, the 'Eureka' effect. The left hemisphere must then provide the critical thinking and step-by-step planning required to implement the idea.

In the profile shown in the diagram we appear to have a person who is left-hemisphere dominant, ie better at planning and organising than at producing radical new ideas.

Some of the most important characteristics of the two hemispheres where they are dominant can be summarised as follows:

Left hemisphere	Right hemisphere
Analytical and rational.	Intuitive and imaginative.
Thinks in terms of logical patterns and sequences.	Thinks in terms of creative leaps and holistic visions.
Well-organised, tidy, punctual.	Seldom at a loss for ideas.
May be intolerant of people who do not manifest or value these skills and qualities.	May be untidy or disorganised and scornful of those who have a high regard for order or punctuality.
May label right-hemisphere thinkers as 'impractical dreamers' or 'bohemian idealists'.	May label left-hemisphere thinkers as 'obsessively tidy' or 'bureaucratic'.

One can readily see how a heavy hemisphere imbalance can cause problems in a team of people who are not 'like minded'. It is important for group members to accept the value of people who are very different from themselves in the ways they think and behave. The special qualities of both hemispheres of the human brain must be fully utilised if groups and individuals are to become effective in creative thinking, problem-solving and achieving goals.

The left hemisphere alone

can analyse, judge, reason and evaluate,

but can never by itself create.

The right hemisphere alone

can imagine, dream or picture,

but can never criticise or develop.

Creativity without development is barren,

But development without creativity is impossible.

One of the most important things we can learn to do in order to further our development is to master the process of hemispheric 'switching', which is vital to the whole creative process. Techniques such as creative visualisation, musical or rhythmic strategies and verbal devices or 'mantras' have been used for centuries to quieten the 'over-thinking' brain and release the flow of the unconscious. Examples of these techniques and the ways in which the two hemispheres may be managed are explored in Elliott-Kemp (1984).

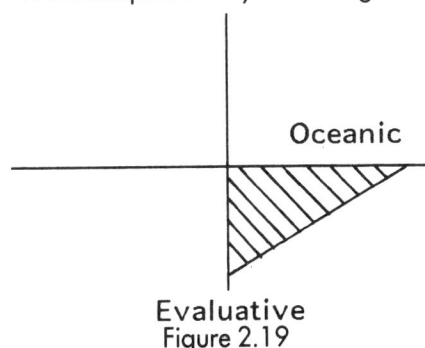

The bottom right-hand triangle is bounded by the Evaluative (objective, analytical) and Oceanic (thoughtful, reflective) polarities. A person who has this triangle as the dominant one of the four is likely to possess the following characteristics:

Figure 2.19

- inward-looking and not particularly interested in the world of action or in other people's feelings.
- takes a commonsense attitude to work and is usually very predictable in his/her ideas and behaviour,
- a reliable colleague who will provide few surprises,
- high on judgemental ability, but may be low on compassion or consideration,
- prefers to weigh up the alternatives carefully before acting,

– not usually an innovator, and may be reluctant to try out new ideas until others have demonstrated their worth.

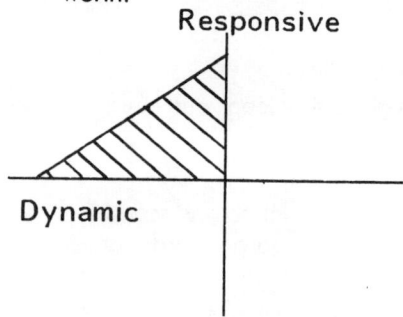

Responsive

Dynamic

The top left-hand triangle of the profile falls between the two leadership polarities of 'concern for task' (Dynamic) and 'concern for people' (Responsive). Those who have this as their major triangle are likely to be natural change agents who are:

Figure 2.20

– outward-looking but not prone to great introspection or self-analysis,
– persuasive and influential among colleagues,
– enthusiastic and optimistic in setting out their views and opinions,
– skilled at developing and maintaining personal networks,
– quick to respond when change is needed but may be lacking in perseverance to follow through a new development when the initial excitement has died down.

The Behavioural Profile related to effective teamwork

One of the most valuable works on effective work teams to appear in the 1980s has been Meredith Belbin's (1981) study of management teams and their success or failure. Following comprehensive empirical studies of groups in action, Belbin has identified a set of key types – roles that must be performed in a working group if it is to be an effective team.

As a result of Belbin's work a large corporation will be able to select just the right 'blend' of different people drawn from a pool of employees on the basis of interviews and personality tests, to create a team of people who, between them, possess *all* the characteristics of the primary role types. Each individual chosen will of course tend to have a bias towards one or more of the key roles, but what matters is that within the chosen group *someone* is capable of performing each role well.

There is a remarkable parallel between the Behavioural Profile framework and the array of primary role types in Belbin's model for effective teams. The Belbin role types can be fitted as an overlay on the Behavioural Profile to fill all the quadrant and polarity spaces as in Figure 2.21.

Behavioural Profile polarities are labelled in capital letters and each Belbin 'type' is enclosed by inverted commas with its key characteristics listed beneath within brackets.

Schools and colleges are not, of course, in the same position as large industrial organisations who can select a management team for a new project from a large pool of people. In seeking to have effective teamwork among staff, therefore, schools will need to emphasise development of existing staff rather than selection of a new group of people. As the whole purpose of the Behavioural Profile is to present a framework for development, it is easy to see how a team of school staff can use their profiles to identify both individual and team development challenges.

Behavioural Profile dimensions in relation to the Belbin Primary Role typology

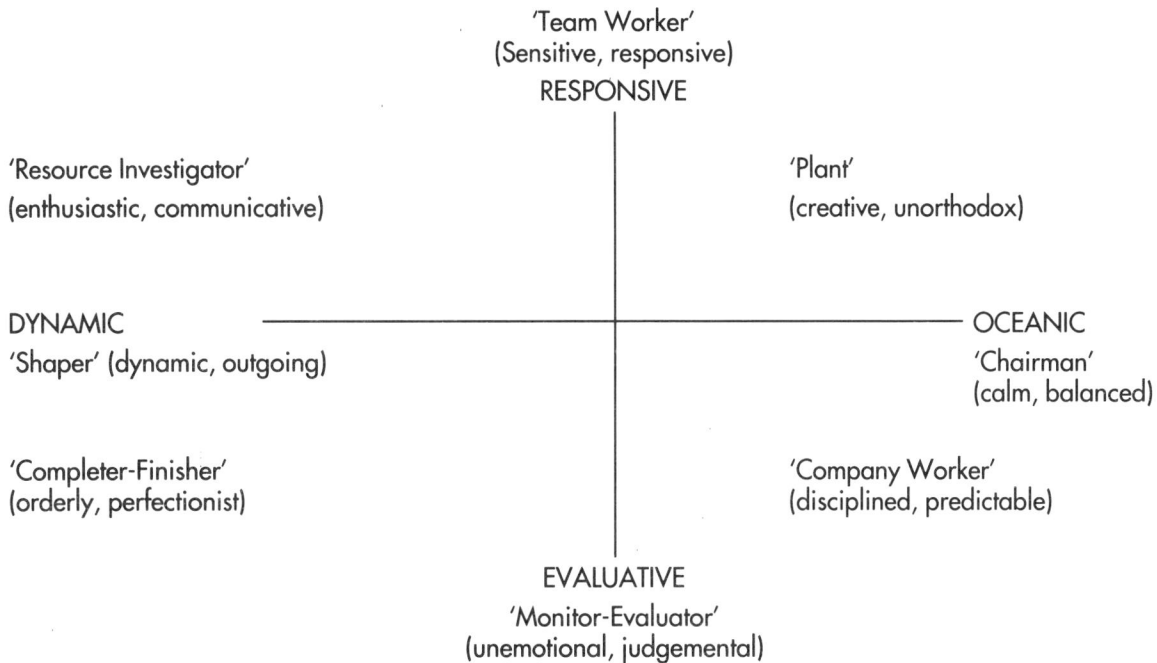

```
                          'Team Worker'
                       (Sensitive, responsive)
                          RESPONSIVE
                               |
'Resource Investigator'        |              'Plant'
(enthusiastic, communicative)  |              (creative, unorthodox)
                               |
                               |
DYNAMIC ────────────────────────────────────────── OCEANIC
'Shaper' (dynamic, outgoing)   |              'Chairman'
                               |              (calm, balanced)
                               |
'Completer-Finisher'           |              'Company Worker'
(orderly, perfectionist)       |              (disciplined, predictable)
                               |
                          EVALUATIVE
                       'Monitor-Evaluator'
                    (unemotional, judgemental)
```

Figure 2.21

The concept of dark potential

In interpreting high and low scores in the four polarities we have up to now emphasised a simple relationship: ie a high score will tend to indicate a strength, whilst a low score indicates a possible development challenge.

But we need to make an addition to this, for there is a sense in which a *very* high score in any of the polarities may signal danger: for within our greatest strengths may lie the seeds of our destruction or downfall.

Each of the four fundamental principles or ways can harbour a 'dark potential', a path leading downwards to a lower level of being: the realm of the self-negating or self-destructive. This is the level of dysfunction, sickness or harmful stress which results from over-reliance or over-indulgence in a particular path or polar extreme. Thus in human relationships a trusting nature is a virtue and a strength, unless one is too trusting, in which case one is gullible. Similarly, the virtues of steadfastness and strength of will, if overdone, will make a person stubborn and inflexible.

We may, therefore, have two different kinds of development challenge – two different possibilities for improving our effectiveness:

- one of these may stem from an acknowledged inadequacy in some aspect of the profile. In this case we shall need to *develop* appropriate skills and qualities,
- the other challenge may stem from the danger of over-reliance or indulgence in one of the polarities. In this case we shall need to control or inhibit the dark potential and develop the skills and qualities which are associated with the opposite polarity.

The acid test or indicator of a dark potential is that the specific need or motive underlying the polarity is no longer within our control but is in fact beginning to control us and determine our behaviour.

Figure 2.22 illustrates the dark potential related to each of the four polarities:

Polarity	Middle Realm Path	Dark Potential (Self-destructive)
Responsive	The need to love and be loved (Organic, Affiliative, Eros).	Over-emotional, rejecting validity of intellect. Over-dependent and anxious. Over-gregarious.
Evaluative	The need for structure (Inorganic, Thanatos).	Rigidity of thought and action. Inflexible, obsessed with routine, structure or symmetry. Stubborn resistance to change. Fear of loving or being loved. Fear of freedom.
Dynamic	The need for power and proactivity (Explorative, external focus).	Over-competitive, Alpha-type behaviour. Aggressive, hyper-calculative, exploitive. Adrenalin-addicted.
Oceanic	The need for peace and contemplation (Inner development, more receptive and passive).	Extreme reclusive behaviour. Selfish narcissistic pursuit of inner development without considering the needs of others. Extreme introversion. Withholding care and affection. Counter-dependent. Incapable of action.

Figure 2.22

Background to the Model

Strong parallels to the Behavioural Profile can be found throughout the literature of management and psychology. Examples of such models include Jung's (1971) four problem-solving types, Kolb's (1984) four-stage model of experiential learning, the four motive systems proposed by Forgus and Shulman (1979) and the fourfold typology of management styles identified by MacCoby (1976).

One of the most comprehensive surveys of such theories is Hampden-Turner's (1981) work *Maps of the Mind* in which these remarkable parallels can be seen in both geographical and historical perspectives. Quinn (1984) in an international symposium on leadership refers to the fourfold typology as a framework of 'competing values', and relates it to significant examples from the literature on leadership and organisation theory. He also offers two possible explanations of why this particular configuration appears so frequently in such a diversity of research disciplines and empirical studies. The first is a biological explanation based on knowledge about information processing and the structure of the human brain (Taggart and Robey, 1981; Springer and Deutsch, 1981). The second possible explanation stresses the influence of environment rather than biology or neurology. Here it is suggested that the human perceptual system is in fact conditioned to differentiate along the two polarities featured in the model as a consequence of early childhood socialisation (Forgus and Shulman, 1979).

References

BELBIN, R. M. (1981) *Management Teams: Why they Succeed or Fail,* Heinemann.

ELLIOTT-KEMP, J. (1984) *Fostering Creativity: a Practical Guide for Group Training or Self Development,* PAVIC Publications, Sheffield City Polytechnic.

ELLIOTT-KEMP, J. (1986) *The Management of Stress and Human Potential,* PAVIC Publications, Sheffield City Polytechnic.

FORGUS, R. and SHULMAN B. H. (1979) *Personality: A Cognitive View,* Prentice Hall.

FRIEDMAN, M. and ROSENMAN R. H. (1974) Type 'A' Behaviour and Your Heart, Wildwood House.

FRIEDMAN, M. and ULMER, D. (1984) *Treating Type 'A' Behaviour and Your Heart,* Random House (Ballantine Books).

GARDNER, H. (1980) *Artful Scribbles,* cited in STORR, A.

HAMPDEN-TURNER, C. (1981) *Maps of the Mind,* Mitchell Beazley.

HUNT, J. G. *et al* (eds) (1984) *Leaders and Managers: International Perspectives on Managerial Behaviour and Leadership,* Pergamon Press.

JUNG, C. G. (1971) *Psychological Types.* Princeton University Press.

KOLB, D. (1984) *Experiential Learning,* Prentice Hall.

MACCOBY, M. (1976) *The Gamesman,* Simon & Schuster.

QUINN, R. E. (1984) *Applying the Competing Values Approach to Leadership: Toward an Integrative Framework,* in HUNT *et al.*

SPRINGER, S. P. and DEUTSCH, G. (1981) *Left Brain, Right Brain,* Freeman.

STORR, A. (1988) *The School of Genius,* André Deutsch.

TAGGART, W. and ROBEY, D. (1981) 'Minds and Managers: On the Dual Nature of Human Information Processing and Management', *Academy of Management Review* (USA), 6 (2), 187-195.

Learning from feedback: the ISIS framework

The Interpersonal Skills Interpretative System (ISIS) is a framework for recording behaviour in a group in order to present immediate feedback.

The system follows the rationale established earlier in the section on the skilled change agent:
- that we need feedback from each other in order to be aware of our behaviour,
- that feedback should as far as possible be based on concrete, observable behaviour,
- that reviewing is an integral part of the development process.

Use of the ISIS framework takes us a stage further than the previous exercises in that it provides us with an instrument for observing a person as part of a group, for example in team meetings or problem-solving groups.

The ISIS recording system

ISIS is an analytical framework and recording system for the study of individual behaviour patterns in social interaction. It may be used to assist analysis of behaviour in real-life situations or in simulations, role-playing or coaching real-life situations in workshop courses.

The system is based on the use of review partners: participants work in pairs, with one partner acting as observer, using the category framework to record the behaviour of the other, who is the participant. After a suitable period of observation (eg a discussion or a meeting), the observer consolidates the data recorded and discusses the results with his or her partner. In the light of the results of the ISIS analysis, the participant is encouraged to reflect on behaviour and feelings and to set targets for future behaviour, which can be reviewed on a later occasion with the use of the ISIS sheets.

Review partners should alternate roles so that over time each one acts as both participant and observer. Instruction sheets are provided to help both participant and observer.

The letters of the acronym 'ISIS' stand for Interpersonal Skills Interpretative System and the method is a tool for personal and professional development designed to help those involved in group or interpersonal work such as teachers, group facilitators, leaders, consultants and counsellors. It can be used in training or accreditation courses and in in-service or staff development workshops. When used by teachers it can serve as a framework for looking at teaching behaviour or for analysing behaviour in a staff meeting or task group. ISIS is founded on the following assumptions:

- effective professional development is that which is goal-based, that is, which has a built in sense of direction,
- in order to move towards a goal it is necessary first of all to identify where you are now,
- this implies having some kind of checklist, or conceptual scheme, and an evaluation process,
- this checklist should be comprehensive yet practicable, and research-based,
- self-analysis and evaluation are important, but insufficient on their own. Self-perception must be supplemented by feedback from others who are preferably knowledgeable and skilled fellow-professionals,
- effective personal feedback is that which is based on specific, concrete observed behaviour and given with a minimum time lag.

Although the idea of being closely observed by a colleague may feel strange, even somewhat threatening at first, the feeling soon passes and the benefits of direct feedback from one's partner can be appreciated. There is no real substitute for immediate data-based feedback from a professional colleague.

The fact that there is a reciprocal relationship between review partners means that each learns to appreciate the value of tact and sensitivity in giving feedback and the vital need for an adequate language of professional discourse, especially in the delicate area of appraisal or review.

The ISIS recording system is based on a framework of eight major categories in this version of the system. The eight categories are grouped according to what would usually tend to be the dominant social motive underlying each type of behaviour.

The categories in the ISIS system are derived from research, drawing on the universalistic work of psychologists such as Bales and McClelland, and specific applications by Flanders, McLeish *et al*, Rackham and Morgan, and Argyle. Readers who are interested in the theoretical background and research are recommended to follow up the references which are provided at the end of the ISIS materials.

The ISIS system has been piloted and refined on workshop courses and school-based work with teachers and school management staff, including headteachers, in the United Kingdom, Thailand and Hong Kong.

There are two versions of the ISIS system. The complete version, which is the research model, and requires considerable time for the manipulation of data, preserves the sequence and patterning of dialogue over the period of observation and produces individual profiles in the form of a two-dimensional grid. The simplified version of ISIS, which is the one used here, has proved more appropriate for practical use in school-based staff development work.

The ISIS materials were originally part of the SIGMA project, published in the UK by PAVIC Publications, Sheffield City Polytechnic. We are grateful to PAVIC for permission to include part of the materials here.

Linking social needs and behavioural functions

The first step in any self-development programme is that of becoming more aware of oneself, and the feedback you receive from using the ISIS analytical system is designed to help you achieve this enhanced self-awareness.

You will be able to reflect on your Behavioural Profile in conjunction with the feedback on your profile of behaviour in terms of the ISIS system. You will then have a clear view of the concrete behaviour characteristic of differing leadership styles and can consciously model your behaviour to fit a self-chosen pattern.

Consider the following kinds of behaviour which occur in social interaction and which are arranged here in the form of a continuum so that they 'shade' from 'affiliative – facilitative' via 'facilitative – achievement-centred' to 'achievement – power-centred' leadership:

Affiliative behaviour
- expressing warmth, support, liking,
- drawing others into a discussion,
- bringing people together,
- helping people to relax,
- using other people's suggestions, or adding to them,

Achievement-centred behaviour
- looking for relevant information or ideas,
- sharing one's own information with others,
- giving one's ideas and opinions,
- making positive suggestions,
- attempting to influence events, people or decisions,

Power-centred behaviour
- issuing instructions or directions,
- criticising other people's ideas or suggestions adversely,
- purely negative evaluation of behaviour of others, making proposals counter to the wishes or suggestions of others,
- ignoring or blocking another person's contribution to a lesson or discussion.

The ISIS system combines these notions of a motivation continuum and highly specific behavioural categories in order to study and develop individual behaviour in groups and contributions to team meetings.

The ISIS categories

On the two following sheets you will find the following:

SHEET A – the ISIS category system, giving the basic category terms and a brief definition of each term.

SHEET B – the simplified recording form, which repeats the ISIS category terms, but is without definition of the terms. There are spaces on this sheet to collect tally scores and totals for each ISIS category.

Note: – a partner's *Affiliation* score is gained by totalling scores for categories 1, 2 and 3,
– the *Achievement* score is obtained by totalling scores for categories 3, 4, 5 and 6,
– the *Power* score is the sum total of categories 6, 7 and 8.

Try to familiarise yourself with the eight terms for categorising your behaviour, and the way in which the system 'flows' in a continuum from Affiliative to Achievement-oriented, to Power-oriented. It may help if you have a mental image of the continuum with the ISIS terms beneath:

Affiliative -------------------- *Achievement-oriented* -------------------- *Power-oriented*

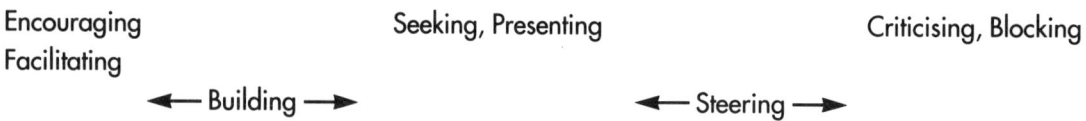

Encouraging Facilitating	Seeking, Presenting	Criticising, Blocking
←— Building —→	←— Steering —→	

A

ISIS category system

Number	Subject Behaviour Key	
1	*Encouraging:*	giving positive reinforcement, showing warmth or attention, active listening; include non-verbal communication (eg nodding, smiling).
2	*Facilitating:*	harmonising or interceding (pouring oil on troubled waters); relieving tension; gatekeeping (bringing others in).
3	*Building:*	developing or adding to others' ideas.
4	*Seeking:*	asking questions about factual data, opinions or ideas.
5	*Presenting:*	giving factual data, opinions, ideas or summaries.
6	*Steering:*	giving directions or making statements or suggestions designed to influence or control the direction which others take.
7	*Criticising:*	making evaluative statements which adversely criticise the ideas, opinions or behaviour of others.
8	*Blocking:*	gatekeeping behaviour which ignores, stifles or shuts out another; making counter-proposals.

B
ISIS category system
Simplified recording form

Number	Category	Scores	Total	
1	Encouraging			Aff total (1, 2, 3)
2	Facilitating			
3	Building			
4	Seeking			Ach total (3, 4, 5, 6)
5	Presenting			
6	Steering			
7	Criticising			Pow total (6, 7, 8)
8	Blocking			

The system in use

The ISIS framework is probably best introduced by means of the 'fishbowl' method. Participants in a meeting or discussion each have a partner whose task is to observe all their contributions to the group and to classify and mark them on the score sheet.

A simple 'tally' system is used, with each fifth score in a category 'tying up' a bundle to make it easy to total each category score:

Score	Total
⊥⊥⊥⊥ ⊥⊥⊥⊥ ⊥⊥⊥⊥ ‖‖	18
⊥⊥⊥⊥ ⊥⊥⊥⊥ ⊥⊥⊥⊥ ⊥⊥⊥⊥ ‖‖‖	24

When the meeting is over, observers should present their analysis of their partners' contributions, using the completed score sheet as the basis of their comments. From experience of using the system the following suggestions will often help observers to become more effective in recording and presenting feedback:

- in the early stages of using the ISIS framework do not panic if you cannot easily classify a remark by your partner. It does not matter if you miss the occasional one!

- relax, and enjoy the process. You will then find yourself more effective as an observer.

- be alert for 'multiscore' contributions from your partner. For example, a simple question such as 'What do you think, Bob?' may score one for 'Seeking' (question about opinion) and one for 'Facilitation' (gatekeeping to let Bob into the discussion).

- it is not necessary to record *all* non-verbal acts in the 'Encouraging' category; just comment on the *fluency* of non-verbal communication.

- when presenting negative feedback, for example on 'Criticising' and 'Blocking', try to avoid making judgements and focus simply on the amount of the score. Simple empirical data can prove far more effective than judgemental evaluation in helping a rather negative colleague to realise what her contribution to a group meeting has been.

- in giving feedback on a 'Blocking' behaviour by one's partner it is necessary to seek the motivation behind the behaviour. Not all blocking is to be regarded as a negative contribution. The issue is whether the aim of the 'Blocking' activity was to help the group (perhaps by blocking an over-talkative or dominating colleague), or just to gratify the speaker's ego or 'score' off a rival in the group.

Analysing ISIS data: leadership and social motivation

When we have obtained data from our Behavioural Profile and the ISIS observation schedule we are now in a position to consider our score profiles and the significance of different configurations.

It is suggested that you work with your review partners to discuss the following issues stemming from your score profiles:

1. What degree of congruence is there between your Behavioural Profile scores and your ISIS profile?

   Did the motivational concerns which appeared in your scores for the two exercises square with the image you hold of yourself?

   How do you feel about your scores and your own image of yourself?

2. To what extent do you accept that particular motivational concerns such as the need for power or affiliation may influence your behaviour with others *irrespective* of the 'rational-objective' requirements of the situation?

   Can you think of any occasion when your own motivational concerns did outweigh the 'needs' of the situation – in the classroom?
       – in a meeting?

3. What motives do you think are most relevant or significant in relation to effectiveness in teaching?

   How can a teacher's need for power and affiliation work in a fruitful way in the classroom?

   Can a pupil's power and affiliation motivation be harnessed to enhance learning?

4. Consider the following hypothetical ISIS profiles:

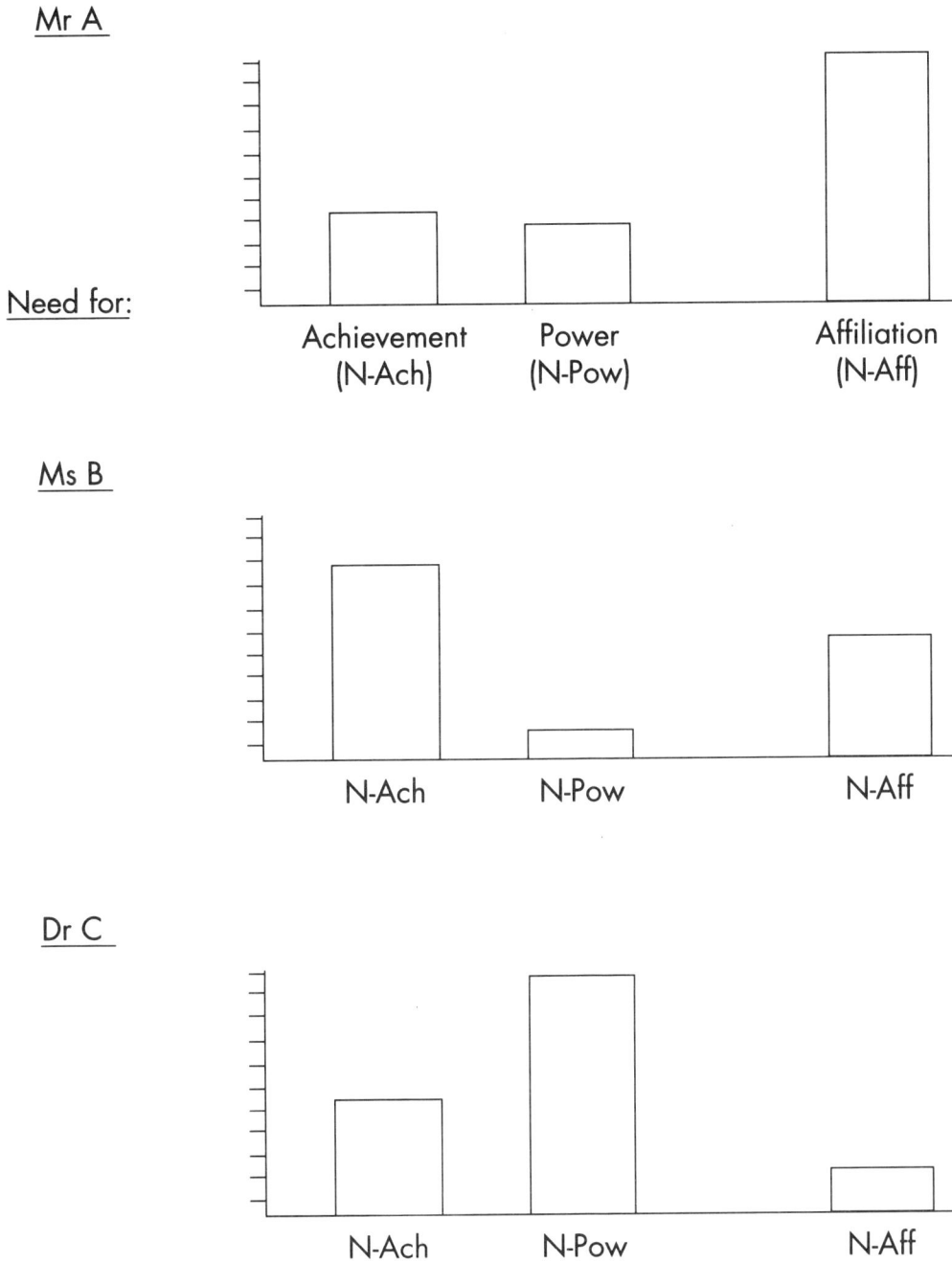

Mr A

Need for:

Ms B

Dr C

Figure 2.23

In what ways are the dominant teaching styles of these three colleagues likely to differ?

How would you expect their social motivation to influence their behaviour in departmental or other meetings?

What would you expect to provide their main sources of job satisfaction?

As a leader or mentor, how would you get the best from these three colleagues?

How could you work with them to help improve their effectiveness?

5. To what extent are you now more aware of your own, and other people's behaviour in teaching or meetings as a reuslt of these exercises?

   How can you make use of this awareness to improve your own teaching, or your contribution to staff groups in meetings?

A model for teaching and leadership

In studying leadership we may find the following model (see Figure 2.24), derived from the literature on group dynamics, an aid to conceptualising the problem. This model can be useful for the analysis of all leadership behaviour, whether formal or informal, and teaching may be regarded as a particular kind of leadership, with simply a greater emphasis on the facilitation of learning than most other kinds.

The model maps out the needs which a teacher/leader must consider in order both to function effectively as a leader and to achieve personal fulfilment.

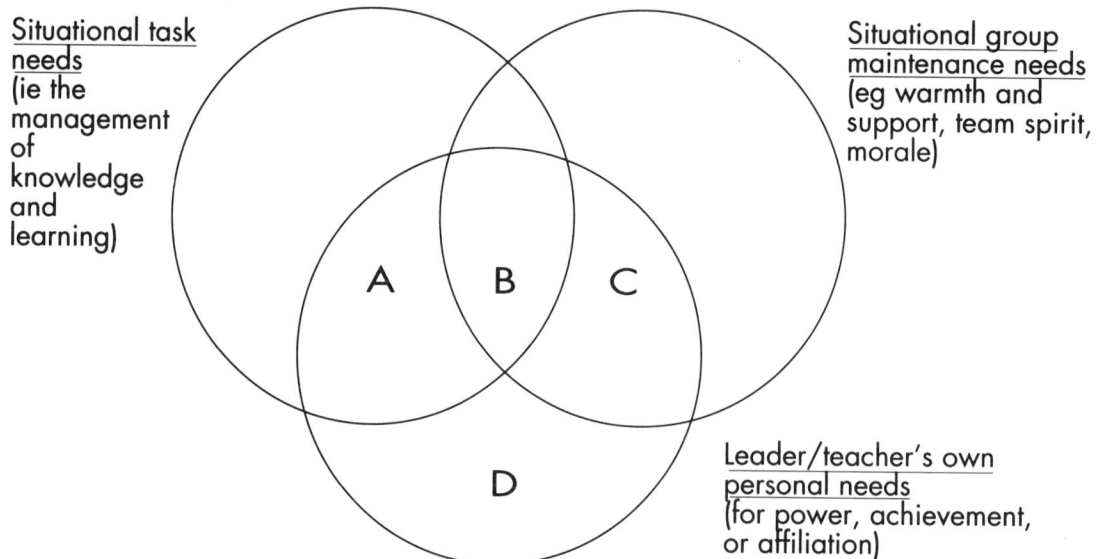

Situational task needs (ie the management of knowledge and learning)

Situational group maintenance needs (eg warmth and support, team spirit, morale)

A B C

D

Leader/teacher's own personal needs (for power, achievement, or affiliation)

Figure 2.24

Leadership is thus seen as a function of situational task needs, situational group maintenance needs, and the leader's own needs for achievement, power and affiliation.

We may define functional or 'rational' behaviour on the part of a teacher or leader as that which is functional for both the situation and the leader – that is, it will contribute to *task* and *group* needs as well as to the leader's own social needs (Categories A, B and C in the diagram).

Dysfunctional behaviour is self-centred: that which helps to satisfy the leader's needs without fulfilling situational task or group maintenance needs (Category D).

A good teacher or leader ensures that his or her actions are channelled into these central areas of the model and are not solely aimed at satisfying personal needs for power, affiliation or achievement. The bad teacher or leader simply uses a situation as an opportunity to gain self-esteem, for self-congratulation or aggrandisement.

The next stage: quality and appropriateness

The use we have made of the ISIS system is just the beginning of our self-development programme. We have concentrated at first on the issue of *quantity* (how many times we asked questions or gave encouragement), in order to raise our awareness of different aspects of behaviour. The next step involves us in a focus on the *quality* (how *well* did we frame our questions or give encouragement) and on the *appropriateness* of our behaviour. Feedback from our review partners will be a vital ingredient at all stages of the development process, and the augmented ISIS model for professional improvement will now look like Figure 2.25.

Increased
effectiveness

Appropriateness
(How fitting?)

J U D G E M E N T

Quality
(How well?)

S K I L L

Quantity
(How often?)

ISIS category
system and
review partner
feedback
method.

A W A R E N E S S

Figure 2.25

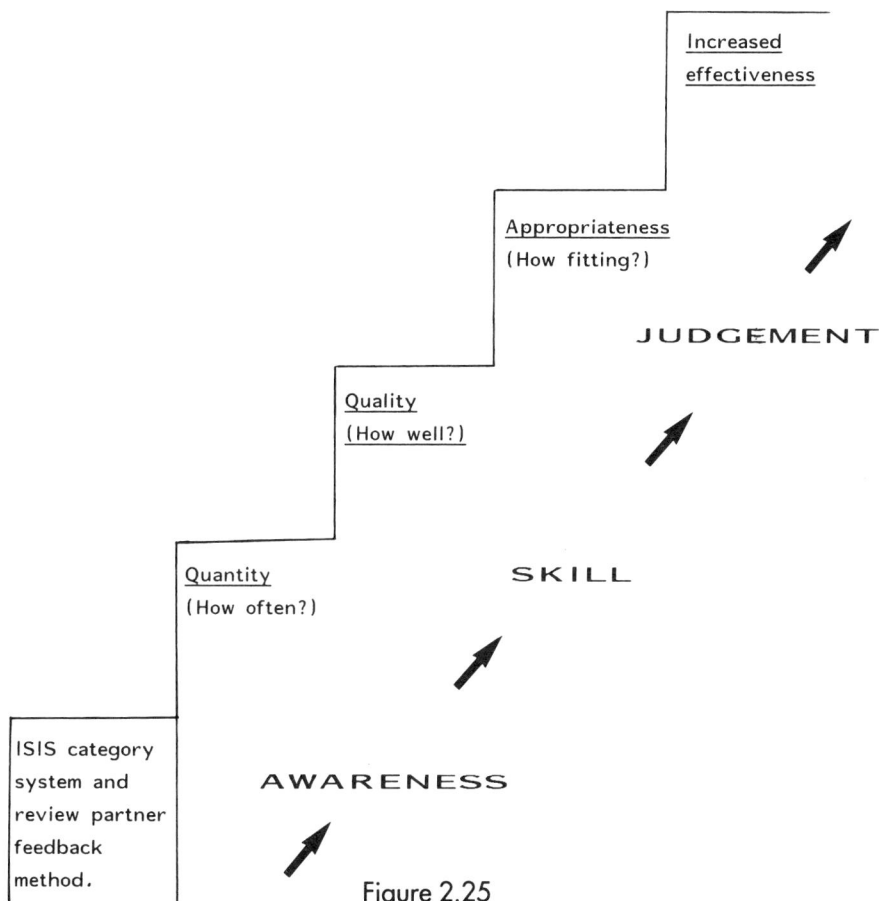

Groups of professionals using the ISIS system are encouraged to develop their own methods for recording the quality and appropriateness of observed behaviour. Some have experimented with the use of video or audio tape followed by feedback and discussion. Others have used colour coding for ISIS tally marks or have written brief notes on any behaviour which was adjudged to be particularly high or low in quality or appropriateness.

References and bibliography

ARGYLE, M. (ed.) (1981) *Social Skills and Health*, Methuen.

ARGYLE, M. (ed.) (1981) *Social Skills and Work*, Methuen.

BALES, R. F. (1950) *Interaction Process Analysis*, Addison-Wesley.

BALES, R. F. (1970) *Personality and Interpersonal Behaviour*, Holt, Rinehart & Winston.

ELLIOTT-KEMP, J. and ROGERS, C. (1982) *The Effective Teacher: a person-centred development guide*, PAVIC Publications, Sheffield City Polytechnic.

FLANDERS, N. A. (1970) *Analysing Teaching Behaviour*, Addison-Wesley.

LAMB, M, SUOMI, S. and STEPHENSON, G. (1979) *Social Interaction Analysis*, University of Wisconsin Press.

MCCLELLAND, D. (1972) 'Toward a Theory of Motive Acquisition', in BENNIS, D. *et al* (eds) *The Planning of Change*, 2nd edn, Holt, Rinehart & Winston.

MCLEISH, J. *et al* (1973) *The Psychology of the Learning Group*, Hutchinson.

RACKHAM, N. and MORGAN, T. (1977) *Behaviour Analysis and Training*, McGraw-Hill.

Effective work teams and process observation

Work groups, like individuals, cannot become effective without self-awareness. One way of raising a group's awareness of its own processes, the psychological underworld of the group which often remains hidden, is to appoint one person to act as a process observer each time the group meets.

The role of process observer should, ideally, be taken in turn by each member of the group. An observer should obey strict ground rules such as the following:

1. Notes should be taken during a meeting and comments presented to the group only when the formal meeting is over.

2. The observer should try to avoid making generalisations, inferences or judgements, focusing instead on concrete, observable behaviour on the part of group members. (This should include both verbal and non-verbal behaviour.)

3. The process observer should particularly note what is happening in the meeting in the following key areas:

   Communication – eg Do people listen to each other? Is everyone given a hearing? Is there a dominant minority?

   Group norms – What appear to be the 'unwritten laws' of the group? (Do people believe these are useful, or a hindrance?)

   Conflict style – How is conflict handled by group members? (Does there appear to be a norm about conflict in the group?)

   Decision-making – How are decisions made? What use is made of voting, trying to achieve consensus, etc? Does any person or sub-group dominate in decisions?

   Group effectiveness – What specific behaviour in the meeting helps the group to achieve its goals? What behaviour helps to build or maintain the morale of the group?

A model form for group process observation is given below. It is not intended as a closed-ended form and process observers should make their own additions as deemed appropriate.

PROCESS OBSERVER'S NOTES

Meeting (Title of group and date)...

Process Observer...

1. Communication

Notes on participation levels:

Did people listen to each other? What were the positive and negative 'indicators'?

Empathy: What evidence was there that group members were sensitive to the needs, feelings and concerns of others?

Any negative indicators? (Examples of behaviour which appeared to demonstrate insensitivity to others.)

Ideas: Who initiated ideas? Who supported them?

Who were the evaluator – critics who tested ideas for flaws, weakness or impracticality?

(Were some members consistently 'initiators' or 'evaluator-critics'?)

2. Conflict

How was conflict handled by group members?

What feelings were expressed?

Can you differentiate between examples of attacks on ideas and interpersonal conflict?

3. Group norms

Use the following table to list group norms (eg politeness, deferring to authority, avoiding passion or conflict), and assess whether these norms helped or hindered the group in achieving its goals:

Norms identified	Evidence	Evaluation (Helpful or not)

4. Decision-making

List decisions that were made during the meeting and comment on methods used to make them:

Decision	How made?

5. Group effectiveness

a) *Task behaviour*

What did individuals do to help the group to accomplish its task(s)?

Name	Behaviour	Result

b) *Maintenance behaviour*

What did individuals do to help group morale and ensure that members felt at ease? (For instance 'gatekeeping' behaviour to ensure even communication flow, positive reinforcement, helping to create harmony within the group.)

Name	Behaviour	Result

Leadership in an age of change: values and vision

This section explores the central role of the leader in developing an integrating vision of the school and its ultimate purpose.

It contains exercises to help in the processes of value clarification, envisioning and enacting (working to realise the vision). These are followed in the next section by an exercise in curriculum dialogue, which is designed to help a school staff to develop and justify their curriculum philosophy or rationale.

Leadership in an age of change: values and vision

Leadership is a role and must, therefore, be examined in relation to the complementary role of 'followership'. Both teachers and those in middle management positions will often tend to have horizons limited by the bounds of their immediate jobs or roles and lack a clear perspective of the whole school. The larger the school, the more likely it is that staff will have this fragmented perspective.

Where this occurs, staff contributions in whole-organisational terms will be disjointed and the work of some may actually be counter-productive in relation to the school-wide curriculum and to whole-school effectiveness. Many teachers will have gained promotion from main-scale level by virtue of technical skills in teaching, a concentration on specific short-term targets within the classroom and the ability to motivate pupils. They may be reluctant to abandon or modify skills and attitudes which have proved valuable in the past. Those promoted to middle management or advisory roles may need help in learning to develop both a wider and longer-term perspective; to see their roles in the context of the whole school without being involved in a competitive ethic where colleagues are seen as rivals and energy is diverted from productive tasks to the building or maintaining of personal empires.

One of the key tasks of a leader, therefore, is to *co-ordinate* and *synthesise* the contributions of school staff. There are two aspects of this key task, the strategic and the tactical. Strategy is concerned with ultimate goals and purposes whilst tactics involves structures and techniques for achieving these purposes. The distinction is that between ends and means.

The tactical aspect of this task requires cognitive, analytical thinking, and is largely a matter of seeing that the different roles and major tasks are appropriately structured and fitted together to form a coherent system. Staff are then allocated and developed to fulfil these different roles and major tasks. This aspect of the leader's work is managerial, requiring analytical, sequential thinking. But it is hardly rational to concentrate on means to the detriment of thinking about ends. Purpose comes before structure.

The need for an integrating vision

The most important aspect of the leader's role, therefore, is concerned with strategic thinking about the school and its ultimate purpose. This type of thinking is *confluent*, that is, involving a synthesis of both cognitive (intellectual) and affective (emotional-intuitive) thought to develop and communicate a vision of what the school should strive to become and which fundamental human values it should embody.

What do leaders do in focusing on their affective-intuitive role of synthesising staff energy and commitment to produce a coherent school policy? It appears that the most effective headteachers in this sense of leadership put much of their time and energy into the following activities:

– they develop or shape a pervading vision of the school and of its fundamental purposes and ideals,
– they develop this vision through a process of continuing dialogue with staff members which focuses on ultimate values and purposes,
– good leaders listen to what others say and take heed,
– in communicating their vision they make their ideas tangible and real, and expressed with emotional power so that they gain real commitment to their vision from colleagues rather than simple compliance,
– leaders thus integrate values, purposes and ideals into forms which provide significant meanings for their colleagues. These purposes then help to give point to the work of each individual as he or she contributes to

the achievement of the whole-school vision,
- leaders bear these values, like flags or banners, in their day-to-day behaviour.

Effective leaders provide models in the ways they behave which are congruent with what they advocate. The examples set by leaders in what they actually do will always be the most potent influence for change. Rhetoric can only maintain its power when supported by actions which are consistent with the rhetoric.

We may conceive of this aspect of the leader's role in two main stages, 'envisioning' and 'enacting'. These stages are not discrete in the world of action, although it is useful to consider them separately when thinking about them.

'Envisioning' is the range of activities involved in creating the vision.

'Enacting' is the process of realising the vision, of bringing it to life.

Envisioning (developing the vision)

What practical steps can headteachers take to fulfil this key task of the leader? There is an inherent paradox here, for, although we tend to think of a vision in holistic, instantaneous terms it is unlikely that a vision will suddenly appear, fully developed, in a blinding flash, like Saul's experience on the road to Damascus. Visions, like fortune, seem to favour the prepared mind.

Where, then, shall we begin? It is not very helpful advice just to say to someone 'You need to have a vision', without some suggestions about how this might be achieved. There will be no one moment when the vision appears but rather a process involving the generation of excitement, energy and enthusiasm, the sharing of feelings about ultimate purposes, values and relationships, mental gestation and calm reflection during which the vision begins to emerge and crystallise.

Although the process is seldom a simple linear one it can be useful to picture it in terms of specific phases around which a school-focused INSET event could be planned:

Introductory phase – Opening statement about the purpose of the event, agreeing ground rules, answering any queries.

Envisioning – a) Value clarification exercises; collecting and sharing data on our key values.

b) Reflection and gestation. Clarifying meanings and consequences of our values.

c) Fantasy: how we visualise our school's development in the light of our shared values. (This is a phase which requires the generation of excitement and energy; it is open-ended and requires appreciative, rather than judgemental skills.)

d) Conceptualising: building our vision, synthesising. (In this phase we group our major themes and draw them together to construct a coherent whole.)

Enacting – Looking at the practical implications of what we have discussed before. Action planning, implementing and monitoring process.

(This phase requires the negotiation of issues such as

- Are we clear about *why* we are doing this?
- *What* should we do to help realise our vision?
- *How* should it be done? *Who* should do it?
- *How* shall we recognise that we are making progress?)

This last question should never be overlooked. Without a clear perception of indicators of success it will be very difficult to evaluate progress or keep a project on course.

The reader will have noticed that these processes of envisioning and enacting are not acts of solitary leadership, but experiences which need to be shared with one's colleagues. This does not preclude the leader's undertaking a period of preparation alone in a personal wilderness in meditation and reflection; indeed this personal preparation is essential.

But the vision, if it is ever to be realised, must be a shared vision, for ultimately it must be the work of others. A vision, if it is to be shared, must be *owned* by one's colleagues, and it is much easier to develop a shared vision together than to develop it in complete isolation and then have to convince others of its worth: the latter way always runs the risk of being labelled 'your vision' by colleagues rather than our 'vision'.

SOME PRACTICAL EXERCISES TO HELP ENVISIONING AND ENACTING

A vision must be based on a strong foundation. One way of laying this foundation is, firstly, by clarifying our core values in relation to the school and its ultimate purposes. Next, we attempt to carry out an analysis of the long-term needs of our students in relation to the society and world they will inherit in the next decade. Finally, we try to create a synthesis of our values and the students' long-term needs:

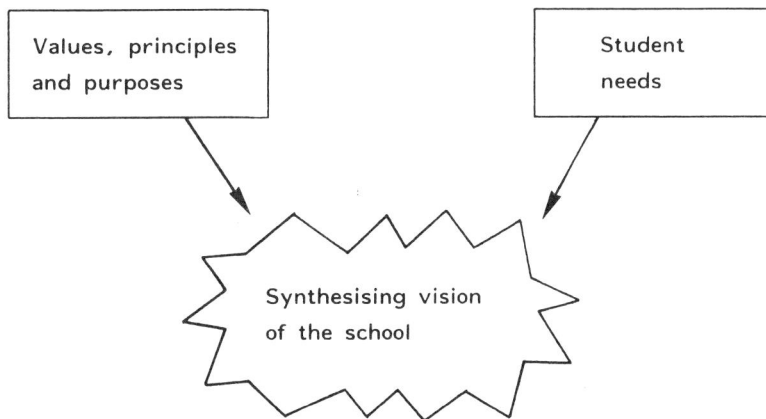

Figure 2.26

1. Value clarification and creative visualisation

This exercise is deliberately designed to help us get away from the facts and figures which may often dominate our thinking about the school: attendance figures, numbers on roll, standard attainment tests, examination results and balancing the budget.

In the process of visualisation we detach ourselves from all the short-term issues which will crowd our lives if we allow them to do so and ask instead questions such as:

– Why are we here?
– What are we trying to create?
– What do we ultimately want this school to be like?
– What is our vision for the school?
– In what ways do we want our school to stand out from the average school?
– Where will our school's special excellence or uniqueness lie?

It will be best to do this as a team exercise. In larger schools a number of teams will need to share their results with each other.

You will need large sheets of paper and felt-tipped pens for each group, and set them the task of drawing a picture, image or metaphor which represents their ideal school. When they have completed their picture they should prepare to make a brief presentation on

a) the meaning of their picture,
b) the underlying values which will sustain the vision,
c) how these values will be visible in the daily life of the school.

It is our experience that Primary School staff will quickly settle down to the task with enthusiasm and commitment. Some Secondary School staff, however, may at first be shocked by being asked to draw a picture. Once they start to talk about their values and feelings, however, and how they might represent them on paper their inhibitions usually disappear. If necessary one might remind them about the iconic power of visual imagery and the part it has played in the history of humankind.

2. Identifying student needs

This exercise is a variation on Herbert Spencer's great challenge to nineteenth-century education, his question 'What knowledge is of most worth?' Once again it is best done as a team exercise with staff, with large sheets of paper and felt-tipped pens for each group.

The group task is to attempt to answer the following questions:

a) What in your opinion are the most important qualities, skills and knowledge that students should acquire during their time in our school to equip them for the future?

(Separate sheets could be used for each category of 'Qualities', 'Skills' and 'Knowledge'.)

b) What are the most important implications of your answer to the first question for the following:
   – different subjects, and ways of organising and presenting knowledge?
   – methods of teaching and learning?
   – ways of grouping and organising staff?
   – relationships between staff, and between teachers and taught?
   – the timetable?
   – In-Service training?
   – communication with governors and parents?

3. The synthesising vision

In this phase the challenge is to create a synthesis of staff values and long-term student needs. This is an exercise which requires a digestion and gestation period before the groups sit down to complete the task of synthesising the results of the first two exercises. Ideally the large sheets of paper containing the results of the groups' work should be displayed somewhere where staff will regularly see them.

Everyone can then be given notice of the meeting to put the group papers together to form a mission statement after everyone has been able to absorb, reflect on and discuss the content of the papers informally with peers and friends.

The statement of mission should be quite short. Its purpose is to crystallise your vision in a form which can have maximum impact. One way of presenting the task might be as follows:

Imagine that we are given just twenty seconds' air time to broadcast a statement of our mission. Can we design a statement which will present our mission within this time constraint?

When this has been completed, the major conclusions from parts 1 and 2 can be refined to expand on the basic mission statement, and the whole then become the basis of the school's policy document.

Envisioning and enacting through curriculum dialogue

We owe the development of this section to the perspicacity of Allan Day, Head of Southall School, Dawley, Telford, who perceived the fundamental parallel between the key dimensions used in assessing school culture (Chapter 3) and similar dimensions affecting curriculum structure and delivery. Allan Day's Curriculum Profile Exercise and other exercises are contained in Curriculum Dialogue *(Elliott-Kemp and Day, 1989) which can be obtained from PAVIC Publications, Sheffield City Polytechnic, ISBN 0 86339 2415.*

The curriculum is at the heart of the school's purpose and mission. But 'curriculum' as a concept can have a range of meanings:

- **the rhetorical curriculum**, usually set out in the policy statements of a school or a subject department,
- **the 'delivered' or taught curriculum**, to be found in the teaching practices and interpersonal behaviour of the teachers. The delivered curriculum will inevitably involve a measure of distortion of the rhetorical curriculum because the teacher is not a machine. The current predilection for metaphors drawn from the world of the factory, and epitomised by the term 'delivery', will tend to imply that the planning-teaching-learning process is a predictable, mechanistic one. But teachers, being human, *interpret* the rhetorical curriculum through the filter system of their values, attitudes, conceptual abilities and social needs. Teachers cannot therefore be regarded as 'delivery vehicles', transporting parcels of knowledge to a given destination – the students. In 'curriculum delivery' we must accept the inevitability that what sets out on this journey will not be quite the same as what arrives at the destination.
- **the received curriculum**, which is what ends up in the minds of the pupils or students. The students in turn interpret the taught curriculum through their mental and emotional filter system, rejecting or re-interpreting some parts and adding or inventing parts of their own. They will, like all humankind, try to make sense of what is given to them.

If any of these meanings can be said to be the 'real' curriculum it is arguably this last one.

Curriculum, then, is not pure information. It is a tension between information delivered by professionals and active learning by a child. Information cannot be delivered without the child's active participation, and, even more, the act of participating changes the information from something external to something internal. The child, in constructing a personal world, is at least an equal partner in curriculum, and cannot be left out of the equation.

If the curriculum is not simply something 'given' for the child, neither is it something 'given' for the teacher. And yet, with the advent of a National Curriculum in which programmes of study, attainment targets and levels of expected attainment are prescribed, the curriculum is undeniably moving in the direction of external imposition on both teachers and pupils. Such external controls must compete with the autonomy of the 'knowledge-worker' teacher and the capability of the school to devise its own internal participative decision-making systems.

The introduction of National Curriculum, therefore, makes it more, not less, important for individual teachers and school staff as a body to re-evaluate the principles on which their curriculum and the curriculum 'delivery' are based. The key issues, for both pupils and teachers, are individual freedom in tension with social control, and an external body of knowledge in tension with the individual motivational systems of the child and teacher. The SIGMA Curriculum Profile exercise can therefore be used to explore curricular issues in terms of:

1. Individual teacher self-analysis and review.
2. Exploration of different emphases between individuals or departments. This could be for the purpose of differentiation, or alternatively reconciliation, and establishing mutual understanding.
3. Envisioning and enacting curriculum policy and rationale; whole-school direction, and consensus about movement in a particular direction.
4. Analysis of National Curriculum expectations and development of a school curriculum philosophy or rationale which will allow assimilation of National Curriculum, while maintaining important school values.

The SIGMA Curriculum Profile exercise

THE PROCESS

1. The list of key terms on the master sheet which follows is presented to participants one row at a time by overhead projector. Each line, however, is jumbled so that words are not ranged in factor groups as in the four columns on the master sheet.

2. Participants are asked to write down each line of four terms as it appears on the screen and then rank-order each term in the line so as *to reflect their own ideal view of the curriculum.*

   Score points should be written above each term in the line as follows:

   4 points – this is the idea or concept in this row which I would rate as most important or valuable in the curriculum.

   2 points – this in my view is the next in importance.

   1 point   – I rate this concept or idea third in importance.

   0 points – I believe this is the least important or valuable of the four.

3. When the scoring has been completed, copies of the master sheet are distributed and participants total their scores for each of the four curriculum elements.

4. These scores are then transferred to the SIGMA Curriculum Elements Profile Sheet by marking each score point on the appropriate dotted diagonal line.

   Each score point on the profile sheet is used to construct a square by drawing a horizontal and vertical line from the score mark to the solid line which forms the boundary of each curriculum element.

Continued on page 63

CURRICULUM ELEMENTS MASTER SHEET

SC-K	SC-CD	IF-K	IF-CD
SUBJECTS	SKILLS	INVESTIGATIONS	PUPIL CHOICE
ACHIEVEMENT OF SET STANDARDS	CONCEPTS	DISCOVERY	PUPIL SELF-ASSESSMENT
ACQUISITION OF INFORMATION	TRAINING	EXPLORATION	EMOTIONAL INTEGRATION
CURRICULUM BREADTH	STRUCTURED PROGRAMMES	RELEVANCE	PUPIL DECISION-MAKING
EXAM SUCCESS OR ACCREDITATION	BEHAVIOURAL NORMS	OPEN-ENDED LEARNING OUTCOMES	SETTING PERSONAL OBJECTIVES
KNOWLEDGEABLE	MASTERED BASIC SKILLS	ACTIVE LEARNER	HIGHLY MOTIVATED
WELL-INFORMED	COMPLETES SET TASKS	INQUISITIVE	SELF-DIRECTED

CURRICULUM ELEMENTS PROFILE SHEET

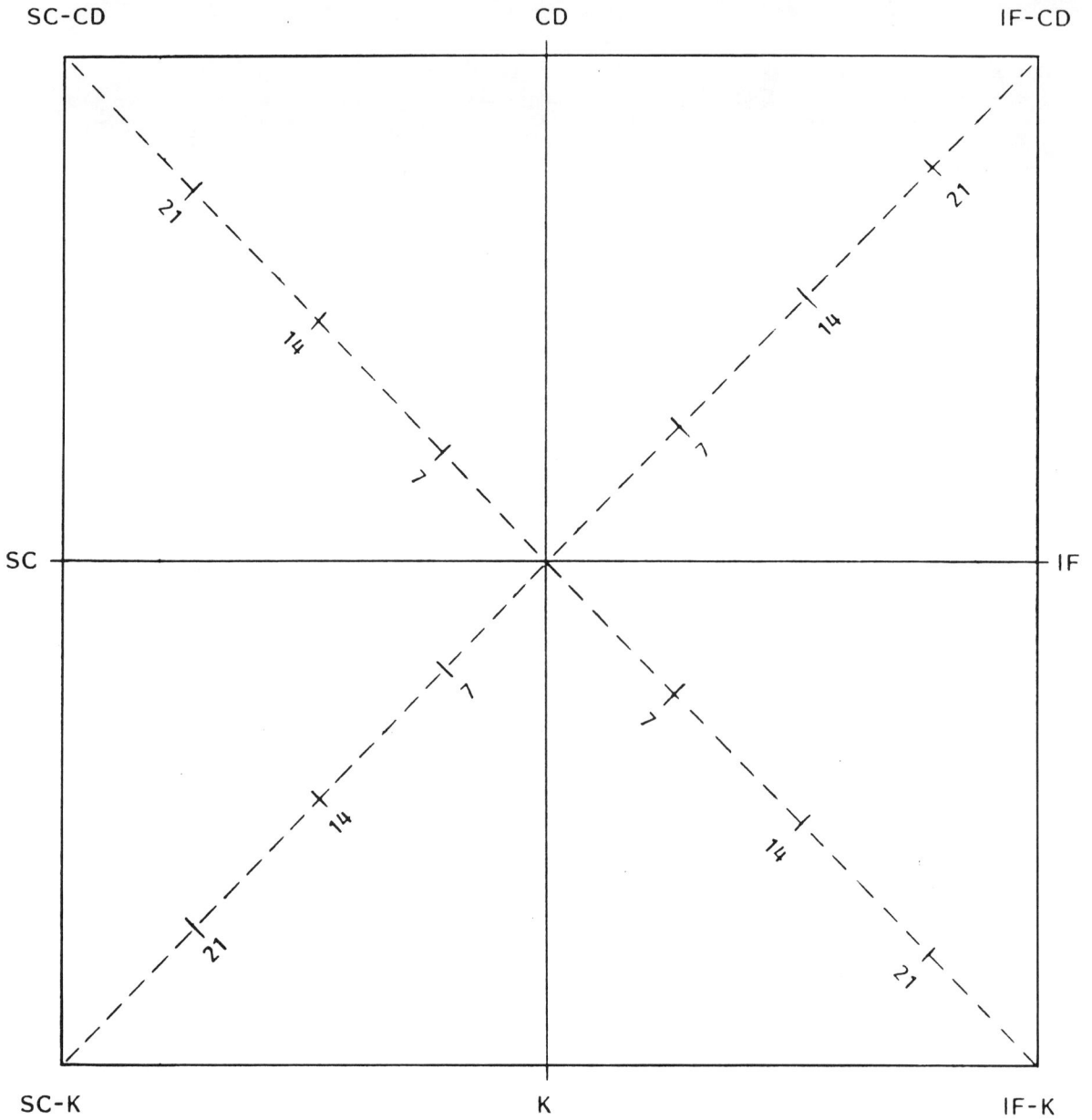

Figure 2.27

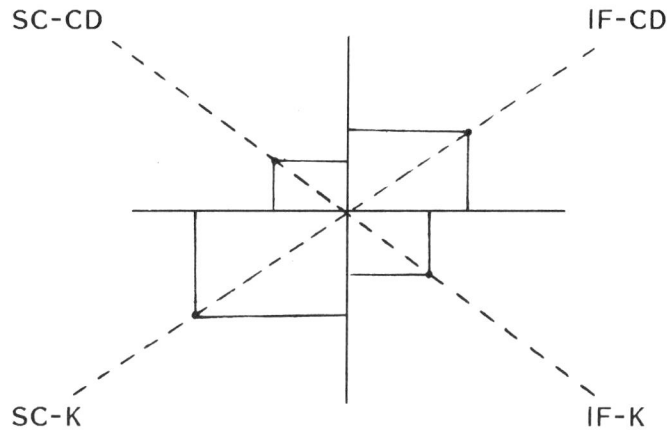

Figure 2.28

5. At this stage of the diagnostic review school staff will quite naturally be eager to compare their own profiles with those of colleagues and friends.

During this period the trainer or facilitator can give out copies of the paper 'Profiling Curriculum Elements: an Explanatory Paper' (given in full, below, pp66–68). Participants should be encouraged to read this paper through relatively quickly. The facilitator should then give a short presentation of the rationale of the system, and give participants an opportunity to ask questions.

The most important overall goal for the facilitator in this diagnostic phase is to assist participants to clarify the meaning of their profiles. It will be with this aim in mind that the trainer moves on to help members explore issues arising from the diagnostic exercise by posing questions which facilitate the process from diagnosis to development.

ASPECTS OF OUR CURRICULUM

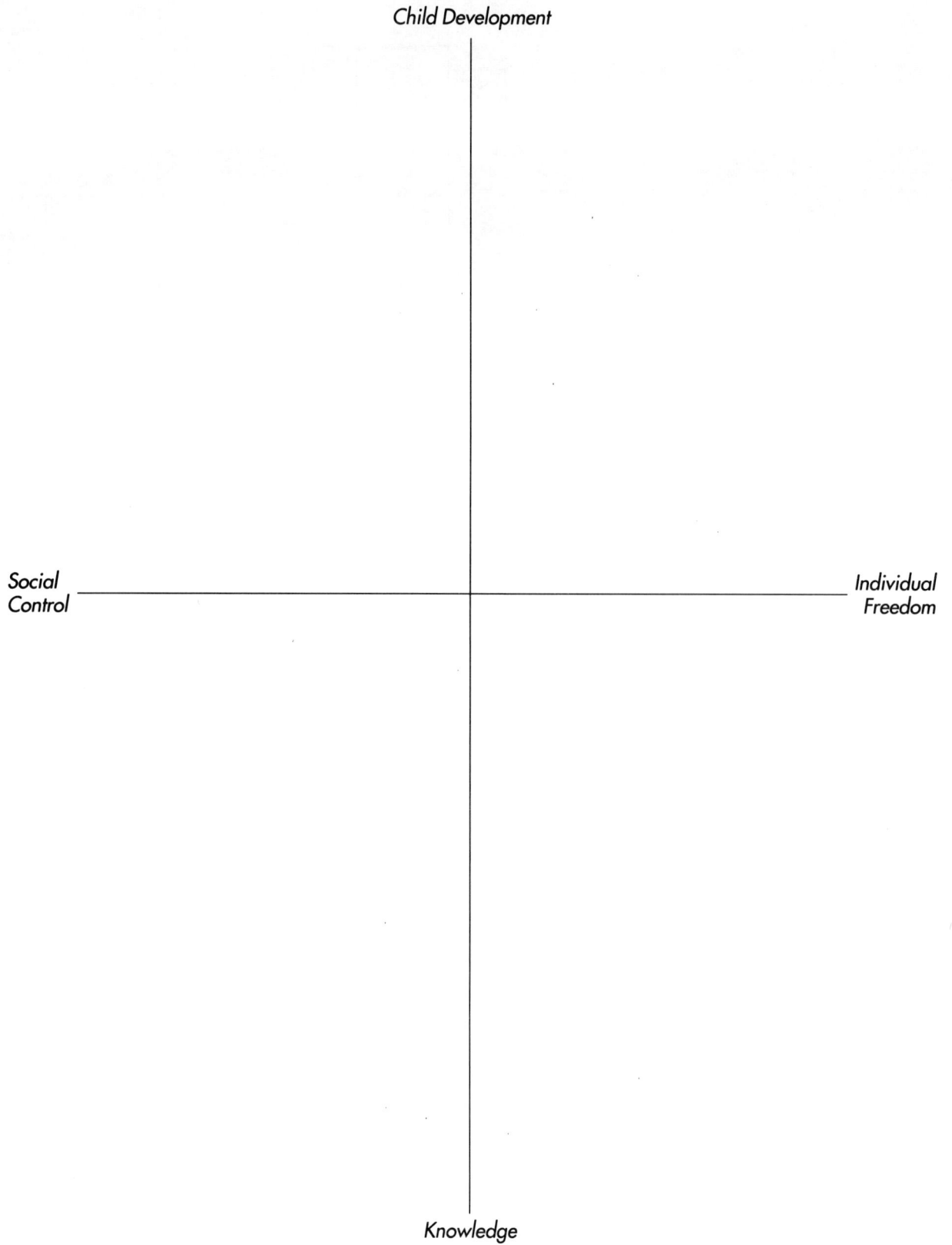

Child Development

Social
Control

Individual
Freedom

Knowledge

EXPLORING ISSUES FROM THE DIAGNOSIS – some suggested follow-up questions for facilitators.

1. The first question to ask is one which has a focus on the specific:
   - What concrete forms do the four elements take in our present curriculum?
   (Use the blank worksheet 'Aspects of Our Curriculum' to record examples of practices, processes, customs, norms and expectations in each of the sections, as appropriate).

2. Staff should now share their data in small groups. The choice of groupings should reflect organisational grouping patterns.
   Some of the issues to be explored are:
   - What measures of agreement do we have in our emphases on curricular elements?
   - Where we differ, can we explore the reasons for our differing perceptions?
   - Are there consistently different emphases given in different subject specialisms, or by teachers of different age or ability groups?

3. This should then lead on to wider issues such as:
   - Can we justify the different emphases on curricular elements given by different staff?
   - Are these different emphases functional or dysfunctional?
     What do you understand by 'functional' and dysfunctional' here?
   - Are there methods of curriculum 'delivery' which can achieve a reconciliation between all curricular elements which have been polarised here?
   - Should there be a whole-school emphasis on a particular direction? If so, what needs changing within the school to achieve this?
   - How do we obtain data on, or measures of the 'received' curriculum?
   - Can we chart the extent of the gap between:
     - the rhetorical curriculum and the delivered curriculum?
     - the delivered curriculum and the received curriculum?
   - How great is the gap between our rhetorical curriculum and the received curriculum?
   - How do we distinguish between a tolerable or reasonable gap and one which is so great that it makes a nonsense of the word 'curriculum' in any holistic or coherent sense?
   - What action could, and should be taken (and by whom) to narrow the 'credibility gaps' in the school's curriculum?
   - How do the school's 'rhetorical' 'delivered' and 'received' curricula reflect the vision of the school which we are trying to encourage and sustain?
     How do we know this?

Profiling Curriculum Elements: an Explanatory Paper

The curriculum is not just about knowledge and skills: it is multi-dimensional, and cannot be analysed without reference to the participants who, by participating, shape the process. There are at least three sets of participants in this process:

Society, which provides a set of norms, cultural values and expectations in which curriculum is embedded, and which trains the teacher to pass on those norms, values and expectations.

Teachers, whose own education and training are embedded in culture, but who also bring something of themselves into the process. Teachers are aware of themselves as partly constrained and partly free agents.

Children, whom society wishes to initiate into its values and standards, but who bring to the learning process their own emotions, motivations, values and learning potential. Learning cannot take place without the active involvement of children.

Curriculum dialogue and subsequent action must therefore inevitably take account of the knowledge, skills and attitudes which are to be passed on, the teachers who are the active instruments in this process, and the child's own motivation and active learning. Broadly speaking, we must consider content and process.

The SIGMA instrument focuses mainly on the conceptual and value frameworks of the teacher and is essentially a projective device to allow teachers to express and explore these.

The conceptual framework for the system is built around two fundamental polarities in curriculum:

- the balance or imbalance between individual freedom and social control
- the degree of emphasis on the child as a unique individual as distinct from an emphasis on the body of knowledge to be passed on.

From these two key issues a pair of intersecting polarities is created, thus enabling one to analyse curriculum in terms of four 'elements' falling between the points of intersection of the polarities:

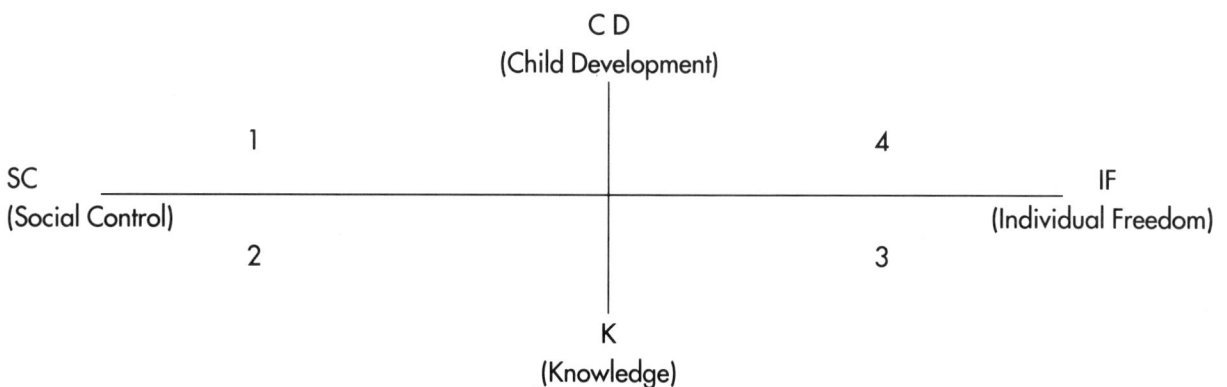

```
                          C D
                     (Child Development)

            1                              4
SC  _____|_____  IF
(Social Control)                           (Individual Freedom)
            2                              3

                           K
                       (Knowledge)
```

A school's curriculum can be seen as consisting of a distinctive blend of these four basic elements in the model:

1. SC-CD – adult structuring of the child's personal development
2. SC-K   – the social control of knowledge
3. IF-K   – primacy of the individual child over the body of knowledge
4. IF-C   – primacy of the child's personal motivation.

The key identifying characteristics of each element are found in the fusion of the two polarities which define its boundaries: thus 'social control of knowledge' (element 2) is characterised by the degree to which knowledge is pre-determined, structured and controlled by society.

Typical components of each element are identified in the following diagram where in general normative factors are emphasised on the left, and child-centred factors on the right. Normative factors include all those aspects of curriculum which are socially controlled and which entail expectations of performance in line with pre-set standards.

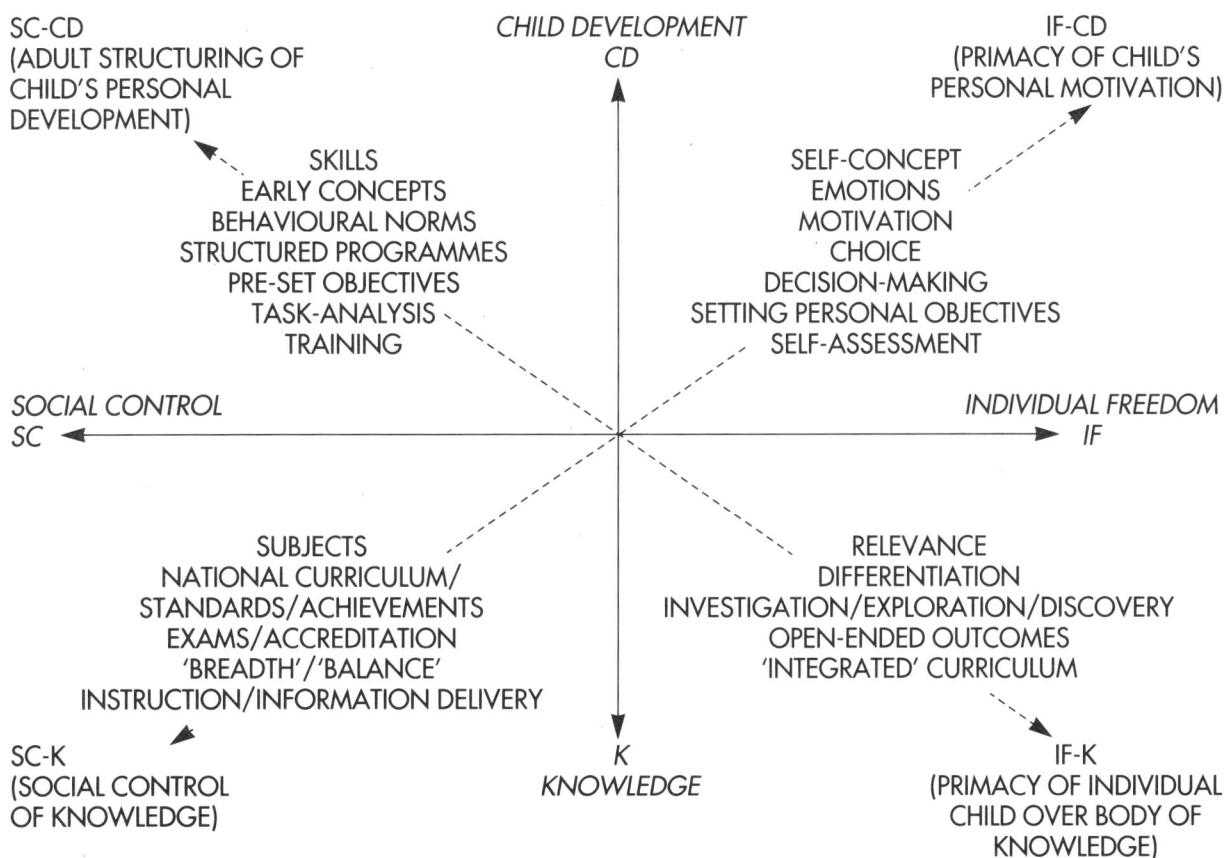

SC-CD
(ADULT STRUCTURING OF
CHILD'S PERSONAL
DEVELOPMENT)

CHILD DEVELOPMENT
CD

IF-CD
(PRIMACY OF CHILD'S
PERSONAL MOTIVATION)

SKILLS
EARLY CONCEPTS
BEHAVIOURAL NORMS
STRUCTURED PROGRAMMES
PRE-SET OBJECTIVES
TASK-ANALYSIS
TRAINING

SELF-CONCEPT
EMOTIONS
MOTIVATION
CHOICE
DECISION-MAKING
SETTING PERSONAL OBJECTIVES
SELF-ASSESSMENT

SOCIAL CONTROL
SC

INDIVIDUAL FREEDOM
IF

SUBJECTS
NATIONAL CURRICULUM/
STANDARDS/ACHIEVEMENTS
EXAMS/ACCREDITATION
'BREADTH'/'BALANCE'
INSTRUCTION/INFORMATION DELIVERY

RELEVANCE
DIFFERENTIATION
INVESTIGATION/EXPLORATION/DISCOVERY
OPEN-ENDED OUTCOMES
'INTEGRATED' CURRICULUM

SC-K
(SOCIAL CONTROL
OF KNOWLEDGE)

K
KNOWLEDGE

IF-K
(PRIMACY OF INDIVIDUAL
CHILD OVER BODY OF
KNOWLEDGE)

Thus, the very division of curriculum into subjects, the imposition of a National Curriculum with pre-set levels of attainment, the wish for the measuring of performance through examinations and reported assessment, are all aspects of *the social control of knowledge (SC-K)*. To the extent that it is seen as important to achieve pre-set objectives, there will also be a tendency towards an instructional mode of curriculum delivery.

On the same normative half of the model lies the element referred to as *the adult structuring of the child's personal development (SC-CD)*. This element is differentiated from SC-K by the fact that it does not emphasise initiation into a body of knowledge. Instead, it focuses on the child's development of skills, behaviour and concepts. Nevertheless, its frame of reference is a normative one, and it will still tend to emphasise pre-set task objectives. Its mode of delivery will tend towards task-analysis and training.

The child-centred half of the model does not emphasise normative factors. Its philosophical base is rooted in a belief in the primacy of the child's own contribution to the learning process. In *the knowledge quadrant (IF-K)*, this means that the exploratory drive and the investigative process are seen as more important than the body of knowledge. The emphasis is on the individual child, rather than the norm, and outcomes are not pre-determined, since allowing self-direction to the child implies acceptance of the risk of the child pursuing idiosyncratic self-directed outcomes. To the extent that the child is to be given freedom to explore there must be a breaking-down of subject boundaries, and teachers working in this mode will favour an integrated, rather than compartmentalised curriculum.

In *the motivation quadrant (IF-CD)* the emphasis is on factors rooted in the child's emotions, perceptions, self-concept, and decision-making. The involvement of the child in her own learning decisions and self-assessment is seen to be of growing importance in the educational world, but it is a tendency which is clearly in some conflict with the view of education which sees the process as one of initiation into pre-determined knowledge and values.

It is not, of course, implied that emphasis on any of the curricular elements in the profile is an all-or-nothing choice, or that any of the quadrants are mutually exclusive. The model merely seeks to polarise some important tendencies in curriculum structure and delivery to enable each teacher to explore his or her own values, and for groups of teachers to compare emphases. In either individual reflection or group work it is worth considering how possible or desirable a balanced emphasis across the four elements might be. Certainly, one ought to be able to differentiate out emphases depending on the nature of the task. It is arguable, for instance, that whereas examination work might inevitably lead to a loading on SC-K, much of Special Needs education might entail loadings on SC-CD, while some Primary school teaching or Secondary school art or drama might entail loadings on IF-K and IF-CD. Differences in emphases can usefully be explored in group work, where they can be justified, reconciled or disputed. If properly managed, this process can lead to a more global whole-school consensus and sense of direction.

The development process can be pictured as follows:

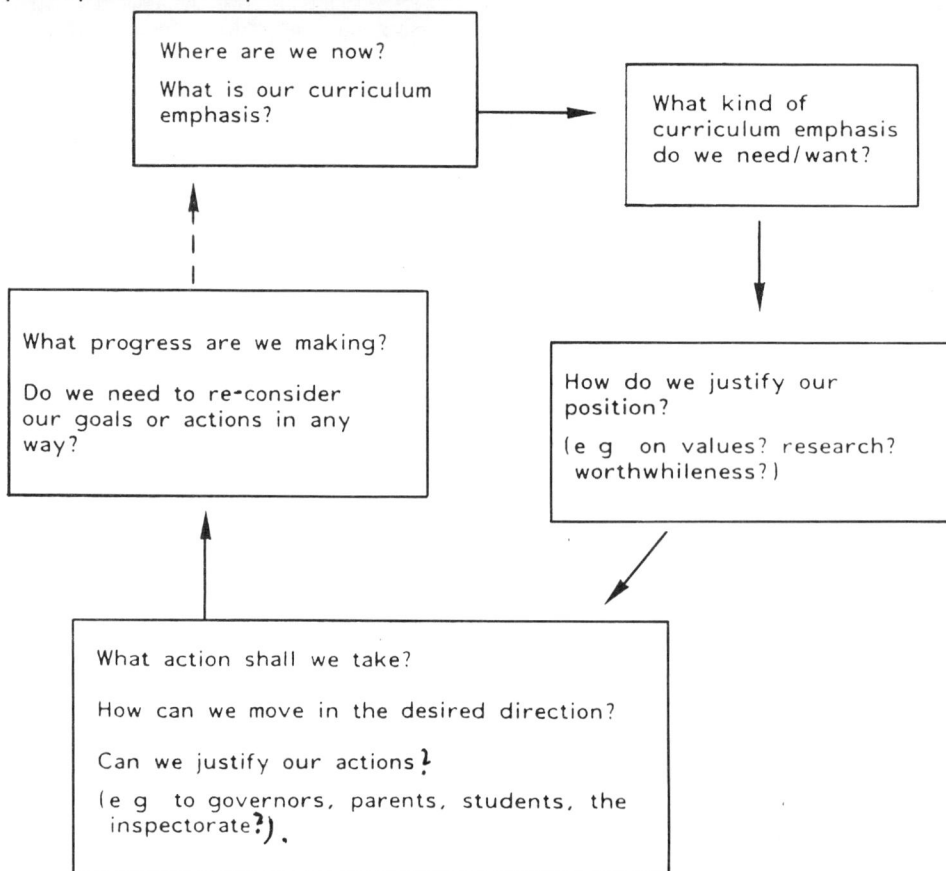

```
┌─────────────────────────┐          ┌─────────────────────────┐
│ Where are we now?       │  ──────▶ │ What kind of            │
│                         │          │ curriculum emphasis     │
│ What is our curriculum  │          │ do we need/want?        │
│ emphasis?               │          │                         │
└─────────────────────────┘          └─────────────────────────┘
            ▲                                      │
            │                                      │
            │                                      ▼
┌─────────────────────────┐          ┌─────────────────────────┐
│ What progress are we    │          │ How do we justify our   │
│ making?                 │          │ position?               │
│                         │          │                         │
│ Do we need to re-consider│         │ (e g  on values? research?│
│ our goals or actions in │          │  worthwhileness?)       │
│ any way?                │          │                         │
└─────────────────────────┘          └─────────────────────────┘
            ▲                                      
            │                             ↙
┌──────────────────────────────────────────┐
│ What action shall we take?               │
│                                          │
│ How can we move in the desired direction?│
│                                          │
│ Can we justify our actions?              │
│                                          │
│ (e g  to governors, parents, students, the│
│  inspectorate?).                         │
└──────────────────────────────────────────┘
```

Above all, the discussion generated in this exercise is an important part of the process of articulating and justifying curriculum values, policy and practices in the development of a curriculum rationale.

When the staff of a school have fully explored and justified their views to each other they will be in a much more potent position to articulate their vision of teaching, learning and the curriculum to governors, parents and inspectors.

Reference

ELLIOTT-KEMP, J. and DAY, A. (1989) *Curriculum Dialogue*, PAVIC Publications, Sheffield City Polytechnic.

The Elliott-Kemp matrix: a planning tool for change agents

This section outlines a method of surveying the organisational field within which a proposed change is situated.

The use of the matrix enables those advocating a specific change to gain a bird's-eye view of where all those involved stand in relation to the change and to each other in terms of the important issues of power, concern and understanding.

The process of completing the matrix enables a change agent group to assess the likelihood of a favourable balance of forces supporting the change and also assists them to plan the next steps in preparing the way for successful innovation.

Introduction

The Elliott-Kemp Matrix grew out of a research project which examined failures in the field of innovation and change. The purpose of the project was to see what practical things we can learn from the failure of innovations and to construct a checklist of 'do's' and 'don'ts' for change agents derived from the literature on failure. Some of these findings feed into the matrix used here and others into the checklist for change agents provided in the final section of the book.

The field of what we may term the 'pathology of innovation' makes enthralling reading. It covers the historical background to human enterprises in every subject area, discipline and field of endeavour, but has been little exploited by those whose work is as practitioners in the management of change. Among some of the most readable and accessible sources are works such as those by Norman Dixon (1976) on military incompetence, Laurence Peter (1969) on bureaucracy and Neal Gross and others (1971) on an attempt to redefine the teacher's role.

The survey of reasons for failure of innovation produced an array of key issues, some of which helped in the development of the matrix which follows. The issues around which the matrix is constructed are:

A. PROCESS

An innovation will often fail because it is conceived as an event rather than a process. The greater the power distance between the top decision-makers and those who have to implement the change and the degree of remoteness of leaders from followers, the more likely this is. Thus, a major policy and structural change decided by a Local or Regional Education Authority such as the move from a Selective to a Comprehensive school system, may easily underestimate the long, and often painful process of transition, which may take a decade to accomplish successfully. At national level, a government minister, with minimal experience or understanding of the situation in schools may decree a new examination or pupil assessment system as virtually a *fait accompli* event. This decision, made on ideological or political grounds, may completely disregard the material resources, In-Service training and planning and preparation time needed to make the change work successfully. All innovation requires extra resources – there is no such thing as a cost-free innovation except in the minds of incompetent leaders who lack the ability to see that the innovation as 'event' exists only in statements of intent or policy. The innovation in the real world will be a process and must, therefore, be managed.

Management of innovation and change implies placing the change in an appropriate time frame to allow for planning, training and budgeting. The use of the pre-implementation planning model in the first chapter of this work, coupled with the use of the matrix, can help to provide a systematic bird's-eye view of change and development within a time frame and consequently help to avoid the 'innovation as event' pitfall.

B. POWER

An innovation may fail because it has insufficient power backing it. The word 'power' in this context is used as an inclusive term and may encompass legal, positional, reward or coercive power, together with influence stemming from perceived expertise, special knowledge or skills, an attractive or charismatic personality, or moral stature, reputation and credibility.

A person who is able to reduce, restrict or limit alternatives available to others has power. This amounts to a person's ability to modify, shape or change another's behaviour. A person may have relatively low power but high influence, so that he or she is not in a position to order or command, but may achieve results by persuasion. Influence will tend to stem from acknowledged expertise or personal qualities rather than position or status.

The power needs for successful innovation and change will vary with the nature, context and scope of the change but the fact will always remain that *sufficient* power and influence will be needed to sponsor and support the change. The challenge for the change agent group lies in the making of an accurate estimate of the power and influence required, and, where it is insufficient, in taking appropriate action to increase the amount of power and influence in support of the change.

C. CONCERN

A frequent cause of failure of innovation is that not enough people care sufficiently about the fate of the new development to give the extra time and effort needed to make it work. The caring, motivation or commitment of staff in relation to a specific innovation is termed 'concern'. Having concern for an innovation implies that one is actively motivated to support it. This support may view the innovation as a means to an end or as having worth or value in its own right. Having concern in this sense also implies that one will act appropriately in working to support the new development.

In the case of some innovations it will be essential to have real belief and wholehearted commitment of the staff group to make the innovation succeed. With other innovations, however, simple acceptance and compliance will suffice. The skilled change agent group will need to weigh up the depth and extent of commitment required from those responsible for implementing the change to enable it to succeed.

D. UNDERSTANDING

Innovations often fail due to inadequate understanding of their purpose, nature and underlying values, or of the knowledge, skills and attitudes required to implement them fully. It will be important, therefore, to have some means of assessing colleagues' understanding of any innovation which is to be undertaken.

At some stage in our analysis it may also be necessary to explore the dimension of understanding in considerable depth, to include an assessment of the extent to which staff actually possess the necessary skills and knowledge and hold the requisite values. (An exercise similar to the one recommended in the section on the effective change agent, but with reference to one specific change could be undertaken here.)

The Matrix in Use

Before initiating a plan for change or innovation it is essential to have some means of surveying the field within which one is working. A cultural analysis such as the one presented in Chapter 3 will help reveal cultural barriers or pitfalls for the unwary change agent, but it is still important to chart selected individuals and small groups and their potential relationship to an innovation and to those who sponsor or advocate it.

The purpose of the Elliott-Kemp matrix is to summarise a change situation in terms of the selected key issues of 'Power', 'Concern' and 'Understanding'. The matrix is a way of setting out the organisational field in a diagrammatic form so that people in the organisation are placed according to how they stand on these three dimensions:

- Are they to be considered as high, medium or low in terms of their power or influence in the school?
- To what extent do they care about the innovation?
  Are they enthusiastic supporters, fairly keen, apathetic or strongly resistant?
- Do they have an adequate understanding of the innovation and the special part each person will be expected to contribute?
  Do they understand the demands that will be placed on them with regard to necessary knowledge, skills and qualities?

We may picture the variables of power and concern visually as follows –

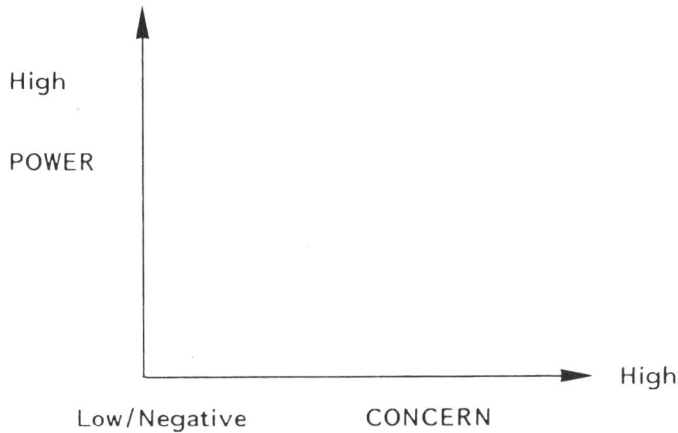

High

POWER

Low/Negative   CONCERN   High

Figure 2.29

Each axis can be viewed as a continuum with high power or concern at one end, and low power or low/negative concern at the other. From this we can construct a matrix with four quadrants:

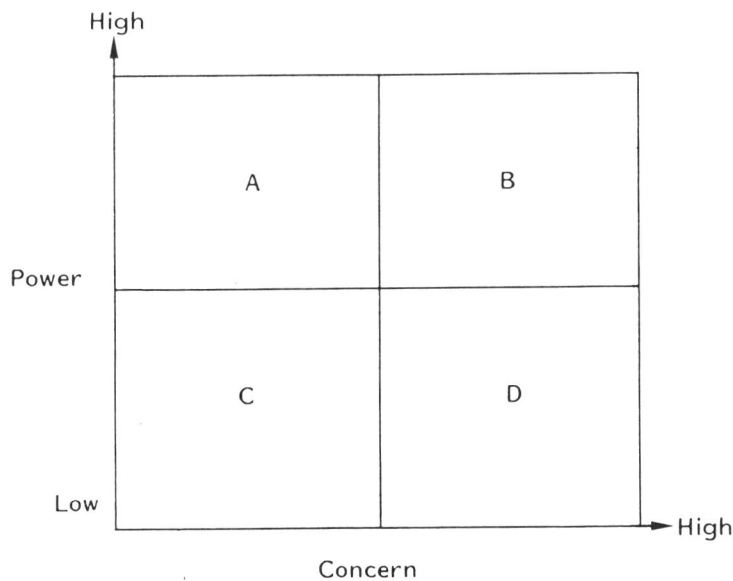

High

| A | B |

Power

| C | D |

Low   High

Concern

Figure 2.30

Quadrant A
Organisation members in this area have considerable power or influence but do not support the innovation.
Quadrant B
In this section are people with power or influence who sponsor or support the innovation.
Quadrant C
Organisation members in this quadrant are low in power or influence and do not support the innovation.
Quadrant D
Here we find supporters or advocates of the innovation who are low in power or influence.

The circle of understanding

Our analytical diagram has up to now been confined to the issues of power and concern. We now add the dimension of understanding in the form of a circle which covers a part of each of the four quadrants in Figure 2.31.

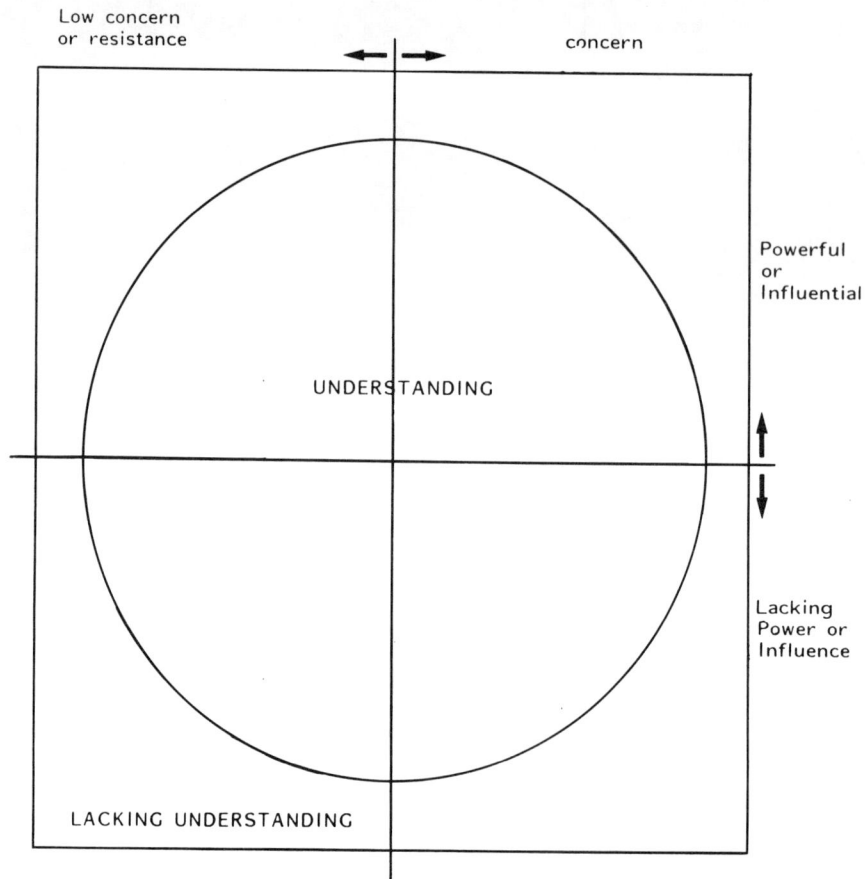

Figure 2.31

School staff who have an adequate understanding of the innovation are placed inside the circle; those who do not are placed outside.

The completed matrix helps to clarify our thinking, to raise many important issues relevant to planning for change and serves as an action-planning device. Some of the questions which are inevitably raised now are:

- What should our priorities be? Since we cannot do everything at once, which things should we deal with first?
- Which are the most important? (What do we mean by important?)
- Should we concentrate first on items which appear to have the best chance of success?
- Is there a 'best order' for doing the things we need to do?

Let us take a hypothetical example of a school where a change agent group have followed a problem-solving cycle, passing through successive stages of problem diagnosis, examination of alternative solutions, and decision-making. They are now at the stage of planning for implementation and therefore construct an Elliott-Kemp matrix for those organisational members who are directly involved in or affected by the projected change.

The change agent group go through two basic activities in order to complete the matrix:

1. List members of the organisation who will be involved in or affected by the innovation.

2. Transfer individuals on this list to their appropriate position on a blank matrix form.

This will often be quite straightforward, but sometimes there may be disagreement among those conducting the analysis over where an individual 'belongs' in the matrix. In the ensuing discussion it will be important to avoid interpersonal conflict and keep the dialogue on a firm rational footing. For example, it will probably be most fruitful to pose questions which encourage people to focus on *evidence* for a particular position, eg –

– 'How do you know that Richard is low on 'concern'?

– 'Can you give us some examples of how Cathy has shown her ability to influence other members of staff?'

One of the most potent ways of using the matrix is to involve all those who will implement the change in conducting the review.

This is the most open and honest approach to the management of change, but requires a group of staff who are not threatened by feedback on their attitudes, commitment and expertise as these are perceived by colleagues.

This can be done by asking each person to place a cross on a blank matrix form in the part which they believe is appropriate for themselves. Staff then lobby colleagues in turn to show their perceived position in the matrix and question each other on why they have chosen this part of the matrix, and how they perceive each other in relation to the matrix. Each person can be asked to mark their own paper with a black cross, and to mark others' papers with a red cross.

When this process is concluded each person now has the opportunity to review and revise their position in the matrix if necessary.

Members of the group then place themselves in a large copy of the matrix, by writing their names, and this is now used as the group planning tool for the next phase of the change management process.

When the group have gone through this process the completed matrix may look like Figure 2.32.

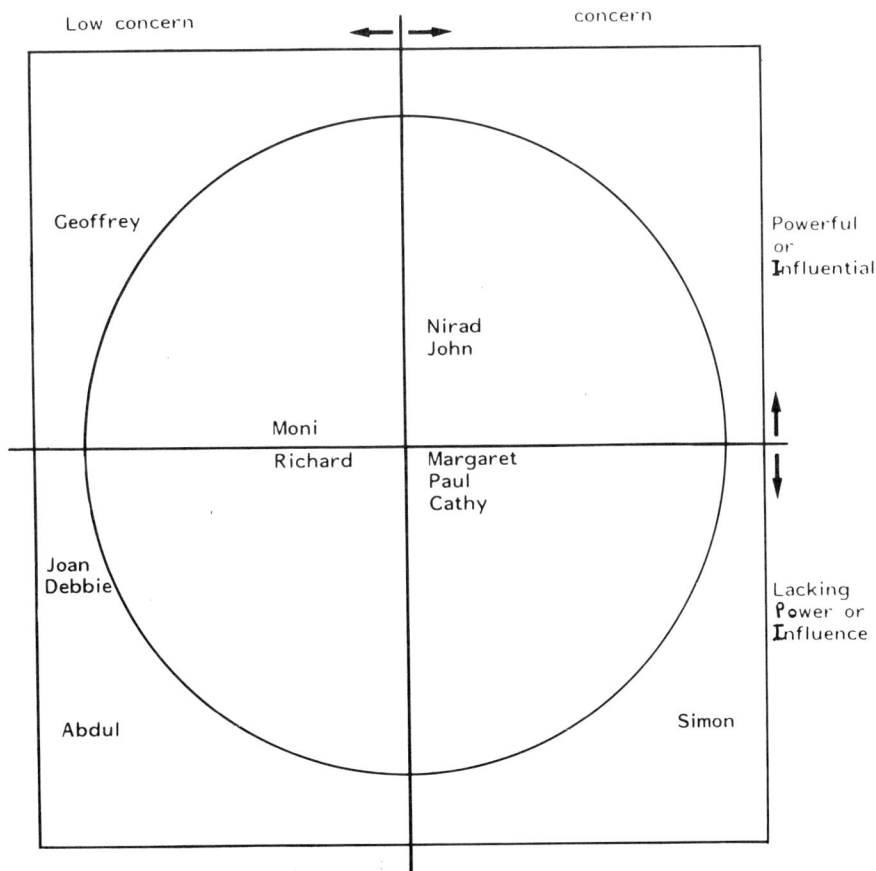

Figure 2.32

In our example the change-agent group of Nirad, John, Margaret, Paul and Cathy have completed the matrix form. They believe that they will soon have the 'critical mass' to provide momentum and energy to implement the needed change, and decide that their first step should be consideration of strategies and tactics for raising the levels of power, understanding and concern for the innovation.

There are four basic possibilities, or combinations of these, for our change agent team to work on:

1.

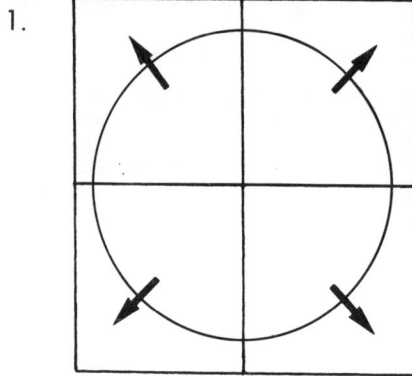

Figure 2.33

The change agent group decide that more understanding of the innovation, the need it will serve and the benefits it will bring, is top priority. They believe that informed criticism is preferable to rejection (or acceptance) from ignorance. The group therefore concentrate first on enlarging the circle of understanding rather than converting the doubters.

2.

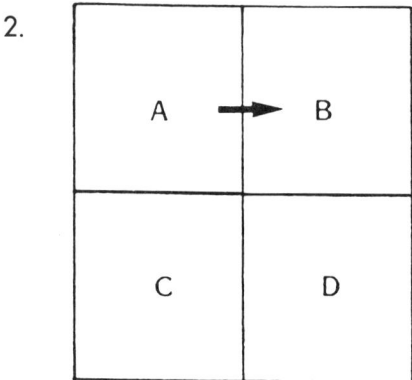

Figure 2.34

Here the change agent group attempt to enlist people in the organisation who have considerable power or influence, but who are not convinced of the worth or relevance of the innovation.

Members of quadrant B must be willing to make time and energy available to talk to colleagues in quadrant A, to listen to their viewpoints and answer their questions. (In our hypothetical example, Nirad and John will probably feel it is easiest to concentrate their efforts on Moni, but Geoffrey is a key figure, being both resistant and powerful or influential. If Geoffrey can be convinced, or even if his resistance can be reduced so that he takes up a marginal or 'sitting on the fence' position, with an understanding of the innovation, then many of the others in both quadrants A and C may follow his lead.)

3.

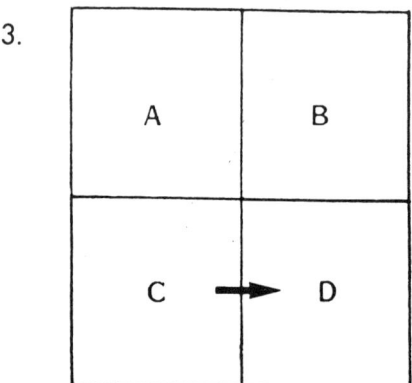

Figure 2.35

In this example, organisation members who have relatively low power or influence but are highly motivated towards the innovation work on their colleagues to help them to understand and accept the change. (One must not rule out the use of quadrant B members to help persuade those in quadrant C, but bear in mind the danger that quadrant C members may feel pressurised or coerced by the efforts of those who are very powerful. Coercion never gains commitment and can only be of short-term or emergency use.)

4.

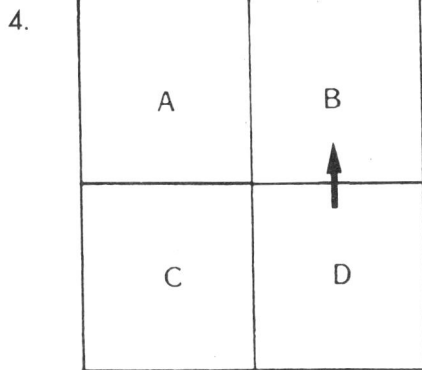

Figure 2.36

The fourth method is often the most important. In many organisations innovation may be confined to 'top-down' change where decisions always come from high up in the organisation. The problem here is how to help committed people in positions of lower power or influence to maximise their potential for achieving organisational change. The emphasis in this case is on synergy building.

Synergy is the extra power and energy created when a number of people cease to function simply as isolated individuals and become a fully functioning group with a sense of identity and mission. The group actively seeks new members, encourages all members to share leadership tasks, and ensures that its own standards of work and behaviour are high. Synergy will be greatest when all members of the group are authentic in their behaviour – aware of their own freedom and of their responsibility for themselves, trying to enact what they believe, and avow their actions.
(See Rowan 1976a, 1976b for accounts of synergy building.)

The Trojan mouse: a strategy for under-powered innovators

There will always be some organisations where all change is resisted by those in key positions. Change agents with low power and influence find that their attempts to achieve 'bottom-up' change are frustrated due to their lack of allies with power or influence. An Elliott-Kemp matrix analysis of the situation might look like Figure 2.37.

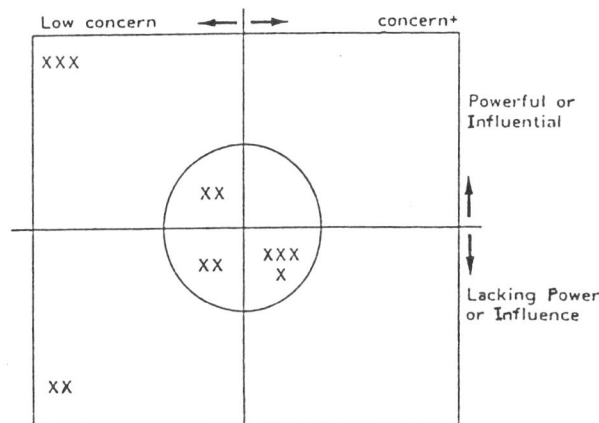

Figure 2.37

The change agent group in this hypothetical example might feel there is little chance of success in persuading their powerful and influential colleagues, especially if there is a long history of lethargy and resistance to change in the organisation.

Their first campaign is to help others' understanding of the innovation they are proposing – to bring as many as possible into the circle. They will then try to raise the level of concern by trying to persuade their colleagues of the worth of the innovation, but avoiding a 'hard sell' approach as this will often be counter-productive. Above all, they will focus on synergy building within their own group to achieve shared values, shared understanding, mutual reinforcement and a sense of mission relevant to the innovation. (Most under-powered or minority groups use this method, many curriculum innovations rely on it, eg Careers and Guidance education, education for social competence.)

But the change agent group may still find that they need a new strategy to help themselves to achieve a breakthrough. Such a strategy is the one we term the 'Trojan mouse'. The basic premises of this method are:

- that often people may resist something new because of its name or title, or because of esoteric terminology,
- that it is easy to criticise something which does not yet exist on grounds such as 'It is just not feasible' or 'It would never work here',
- that people's understanding can be enhanced and fears reduced if they have the chance to see an innovation in action, even on a very small scale,
- that sometimes it may be better to talk about an 'experiment' rather than an innovation: an experiment is more tentative, and implies that changes will not be made unless their value can be demonstrated by the experiment. An experiment also has small-scale connotations, rather than threatening organisation-wide disturbance.

The Trojan mouse approach to innovation is an entering-wedge strategy which disguises the thin end of the wedge in order to increase its chances of effectiveness. (Change agents who make use of this strategy of course have to confront the ethics of using a measure of deception in order to gain a platform for the innovation: the eternal dilemma of whether worthy ends can justify the use of somewhat questionable means.)

The Trojan mouse strategy involves identifying the essential core of the desired change and concentrating all efforts on the design of a small-scale version. The scaled-down 'mouse' should embody all the key principles and values of the original innovation and in its miniaturised form will be used to spread a 'good infection' in the school. An example of this would be a change agent group who mount an experimental short course with selected participants, taught by a small group of highly competent, committed staff. The course would have limited objectives and be so carefully planned and mounted that its success would be virtually certain. This initial thrust would be used as a demonstration model to help others understand its value and practicality, and consequently as a launching pad to help mount more and similar courses as others perceive its worth. Eventually these short courses would be linked together to form a coherent whole (the original innovation).

At the beginning of this entering-wedge strategy the Trojan mouse was carefully fitted into the existing structures of the organisation in order to cause the minimum amount of disturbance. By now, however, the innovation will be sufficiently successful to require its own structure among the other accepted organisational structures. The very fact that it is there endows it with a kind of territorial right, and if the change agent group have succeeded in enlisting the support of any powerful or influential members they are well on the way to longer-term success.

References

DIXON, N (1976) *On the Psychology of Military Incompetence*, Jonathan Cape.

GROSS, N. GIACQUINTA, J. and BERNSTEIN M. (1971) *Implementing Organisational Innovations*, Harper & Row.

PETER, L.J. and HULL, R. (1969) *The Peter Principle*, Souvenir Press.

ROWAN, J. (1976a) *Ordinary Ecstasy*, Routledge and Kegan Paul.

ROWAN, J. (1976b) *The Power of the Group*, Davis-Paynter.

The Organisational Context

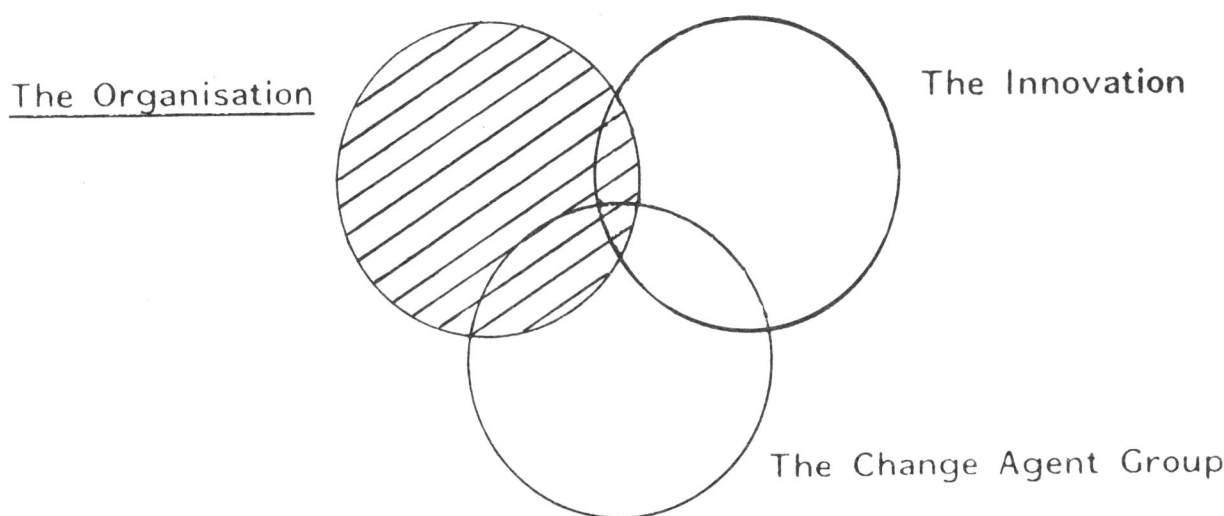

The Organisation   The Innovation

The Change Agent Group

Figure 3.1

This chapter contains two sections which focus on aspects of the whole organisation.

It contains a section on the culture of the school viewed as a configuration of four cultural 'elements', each of which has a part to play according to the challenges or problems which a school may face. This is followed by an instrument for school-based review which provides materials for an assessment of development needs at the whole-school level and a process guide for following up the review phase.

Exploring the culture of the school

Change and development efforts which focus exclusively on narrow, discrete task projects often founder because of the inhibiting effect of the organisation's culture – a blend of norms, values, customary practices and management styles. There is now a wealth of contemporary research which underlines the importance of culture as a key contributor to organisational effectiveness: a culture within which a positive attitude to change and development is engendered seems to be an essential pre-requisite for the modern school or college.

Holistic concepts such as 'climate' or 'culture' stem from approaches which are more anthropological rather than psychological in their academic origins. Since the late nineteen-seventies there has been a remarkable growth in research and writing on the culture of organisations, stemming possibly from Western interest in Japanese organisations and the belief that the key differences between Eastern and Western approaches to organisation and management lie less in design or formal structural factors such as organisation charts and location of authority, and more in cultural influences. In the nineteen-eighties the growth of interest in the culture of organisations has spread from a narrow readership within academic circles to a much wider audience among professionals with an interest in organisational life. Some of these works have even achieved the status of 'best-sellers' (eg Deal and Kennedy, 1982; Peters and Waterman, 1982).

The system used for diagnosing a school's culture in this chapter is derived from *Improving the Culture of your Organisation*, produced by PAVIC Publications, Sheffield City Polytechnic, (UK). The complete diagnostic system and manual are obtainable from PAVIC at the Polytechnic.

A number of writers have developed typologies for analysing and comparing the cultures of individual organisations (Harrison, 1972; Handy 1986; Boisot 1987). The SIGMA system makes use of pure types but sees each 'type' as an element in the organisation which will always be present: it is the *amount* of each element in an organisation which determines its culture.

This notion of 'elements' within a culture is analogous to that of 'ingredients' in a stew or curry. Different cooks may use the same basic ingredients but will produce very different results depending on the *amount* of each ingredient which they use.

In assessing the culture of the school we shall need to involve all the staff, or, if this is not feasible, a representative cross-section. Each member of the organisation brings his or her unique blend of knowledge, skills, attitudes and qualities, and will have a unique perspective of the organisation and its problems and potentialities. The 'truth' about an organisation will always be an aggregate of individual perspectives; meaning is seen as constructed from the experience of persons working within the organisation.

But in order to share and compare meanings it is necessary to have shared concepts and terminology. From the literature on organisation theory the key concepts of 'control' and 'freedom', 'person' and 'role' are seen as central to the understanding of organisational experience and behaviour, and these concepts form the heart of the conceptual model used here. The diagnostic instrument is then derived from this model, and members of an organisation are helped to clarify and express their perceptions of the school or college by means of a matrix diagram which is built up from their own perspectives on the organisation.

The materials which follow consist of a trainer's checklist and instruction sheets, worksheets and an explanatory handout reading for participants.

Trainer checklist and process guide for exploring the culture of the school

1. Explain the purpose of the exercise and the important part played by the culture of an organisation in influencing change and development efforts.

2. Form groups of 2-4 people.

3. Give out sheets: 'A Cultural Profile of your School', 'Examples of the Four Elements in Organisational Life', and 'Profile Sheet for Organisational Culture Diagnosis'.

4. Explain what the group task involves, using the sheets as a guide, and answer any queries.

5. Allow time for groups to complete the task (up to 30 minutes).

6. Encourage small groups to combine to form larger groups of 6-8 persons, and share and discuss their profiles of the school. (Some important issues to explore at an appropriate time are 'How do we feel about sharing our perceptions of the school?' and 'Can we be open and honest in our communication with each other?' People's responses to these questions are in themselves good indicators of the type of culture which predominates in the school.)

7. Give out the 'Handout Reading on School Culture' and allow time for participants to read and ask questions. (Alternatively give a presentation or lecturette based on the handout, followed by a question and answer period.)

8. Give out the worksheet 'Aspects of my Organisation' and ask groups to discuss and then record findings on what they believe are the aspects of each element within their school. They should use the blank worksheet 'Aspects of my Organisation' to record examples of practices, processes, customs, norms, rules and regulations in each of the sections, as appropriate. These examples should be concrete and specific: the more staff learn to avoid using vague or abstract terms here the easier it will be to work on developing the kind of culture which people feel they need.

9. The trainer can now encourage each group to focus on issues such as:

   - *What measure of agreement do we have in our diagnosis of the organisation?*
   - *Where we differ, can we explore the reasons for our differing perceptions?*
   - *Can we identify agreed items in each of the four element' quadrants? (processes, practices, etc.)*

- *In what ways are these items functional or helpful?*
- *For whom are they functional?*
- *In what ways are these items dysfunctional or unhelpful?*

(An alternative approach is to ask participants after each question: 'What do you mean by functional/dysfunctional?')

10. At this stage the facilitator should bring together the conclusions of the different groups and encourage members to look for common ground. Differences in conclusions should not be ignored or glossed over: very often these differences can provide some important clues to competing sub-cultures or ideologies within the school. Some examples of questions that may be posed here are:

How did this particular factor arise?

What need did it originally serve?

Can we justify its presence now?

What alternatives are there?

What are the advantages and disadvantages of each alternative?

An alternative process to that outlined above is to use what we term the M-I-R approach. After completing the 'Aspects of my Organisation' sheet, members are asked to place one of the letters 'M', 'I' or 'R' after each item on their sheet to represent the following:

M – (Maintain) This is something I value, or believe necessary. I should like to keep it just as it is now.

I – (Increase) I believe this is valuable or useful, but we do not have enough of it. I should therefore like to increase it.

R – (Reduce) We have too much of this in my opinion. I should like us to reduce it, or even eliminate it, if feasible.

When this is done the leader or facilitator may collect members' views in tabulated form to use the data-feedback method to initiate the development process. Alternatively, participants may be asked to share data in small groups, where they are encouraged to lobby colleagues and form coalitions around particular issues.

The facilitator's choice of method here will probably hinge on two factors. The first of these is whether he or she is more comfortable within a firm structure, and being in control of both process and pace, or whether one's taste is for the heady enthusiasm of a group which itself assumes leadership roles, including managing the process. The other factor is inevitably the size of the whole group: we have found it possible to use the second approach effectively with up to twenty-four participants, but the larger the group the more some building in of structure is required.

It is, of course, possible to achieve a compromise by encouraging people to work freely within chosen groups and then working with them to develop a co-ordinating function. Cross-group communication can be helped through posters, noticeboards, position statements or newssheets.

Where a school staff have expressed a strong preference for a culture weighted on the right side of the model (ie Job-Freedom and Person-Freedom) it can be pointed out that these above methods of working to communicate our views and negotiate change are in fact doing the very things we wish to encourage in the culture of the school.

The trainer or facilitator may then remind the group of these characteristics by drawing to their attention once more the list of examples given under Job-Freedom and Person-Freedom on the handout sheet.

11. This stage is one of contract building, where staff agree to help develop the school's culture in a particular direction. This may take much time and effort, but without focusing on this issue it is unlikely that major development will occur.

The most straightforward approach is to seek agreement on the different items under two headings:

Things we agree to do	Things we agree to avoid
1.	1.
2.	2.
3.	3.
4.	4.
5. etc.	5. etc.

12. Finally, it will be necessary to involve everyone in the monitoring process and agree a date for reviewing progress. The development of a school's culture will never, of course, be completed. It is a continuing process which must be monitored and managed, but it is well worth the effort as the culture of the school is possibly the most important contributor to school effectiveness.

HANDOUT 1

A Cultural Profile of your School

In the SIGMA organisational diagnosis system all organisations are viewed in terms of four basic elements. These are:

1. Person-Control (PC)
2. Job-Control (JC)
3. Job-Freedom (JF)
4. Person-Freedom (PF)

All organisations will have a 'mix' of all four elements, but schools will differ from each other in the relative proportions of each element in the school.

In constructing the cultural profile of your school you are invited to work in small groups (2-4 people). Your task in these groups is firstly to study the sheet titled 'Examples of the four elements in organisational life' (Handout 2) on page 82. This sheet lists common characteristics of each of the four elements above. Discuss in your group which of the four elements you perceive to be the dominant ones in the way your school operates, and which elements play only a minor part.

Then construct a pictorial profile of how your group sees the school, using the SIGMA Organisational Profile Sheet. This sheet is completed by constructing squares of an appropriate size for each of the four elements. A large square indicates that in the eyes of your group it is a dominant element. A small square will indicate this is a minor element, playing a relatively small part in the life of the school.

Each element in your profile should be given an estimated score on the appropriate dotted line on the profile sheet (Handout 3). This point then determines the corner of the square for each element. An example of a completed profile sheet can be found as Figure 1 (below).

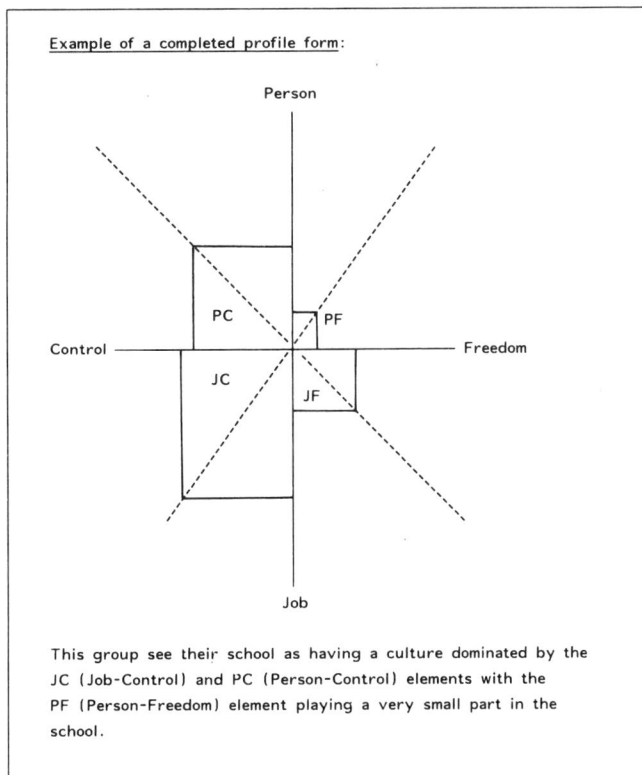

Example of a completed profile form:

This group see their school as having a culture dominated by the JC (Job-Control) and PC (Person-Control) elements with the PF (Person-Freedom) element playing a very small part in the school.

Figure 1

Examples of the four elements in organisational life

PERSON-CONTROL (PC)

Strong, decisive leadership.

Close supervision, tight control. Competitive climate.

Security stemming from leader's ability to establish clear policy directives and to handle major problems.

Emphasis on loyalty to the leader.

Ask the boss before making a decision.

Danger of dependency on leader(s).

PERSON-FREEDOM (PF)

High independence and self-reliance.

Mastery of informal channels of communication (the grapevine).

Shared leadership without reliance on formal structures.

Respect based on expertise or skills.

Security stemming from confidence in self and colleagues.

Little importance attached to status, rank or title.

Contempt for red tape or bureaucratic inertia.

More enthusiasm for experiment and innovation than for permanence and stability.

Tell others, including boss, after making a decision.

JOB-CONTROL (JC)

Preference for written communication.

Emphasis on hierarchy and status derived from position in the hierarchy.

Clear guidelines, standing instructions and responsibilities.

Standard procedures laid down for common problems.

Security stemming from the orderly framework provided.

Red-tape, routine procedures often too ponderous or time-consuming.

May be rigid rather than adaptable.

Emphasis on loyalty to the system and adherence to policy and regulations.

Roles carefully drawn up (eg job descriptions emphasised).

Tendency to 'go by the book'.

Consult the rules before making a decision.

JOB-FREEDOM (F)

Collaborative ethic, emphasis on teamwork.

Project groupings cut across formal department boundaries.

Willingness to accept shared leadership.

Loyalty to team and colleagues.

Security stemming from strong team spirit.

Respect based on contribution to achieving group tasks or goals.

Adaptable to change and new challenges.

Consult the team before making a decision.

Profile sheet for SIGMA organisational culture diagnosis

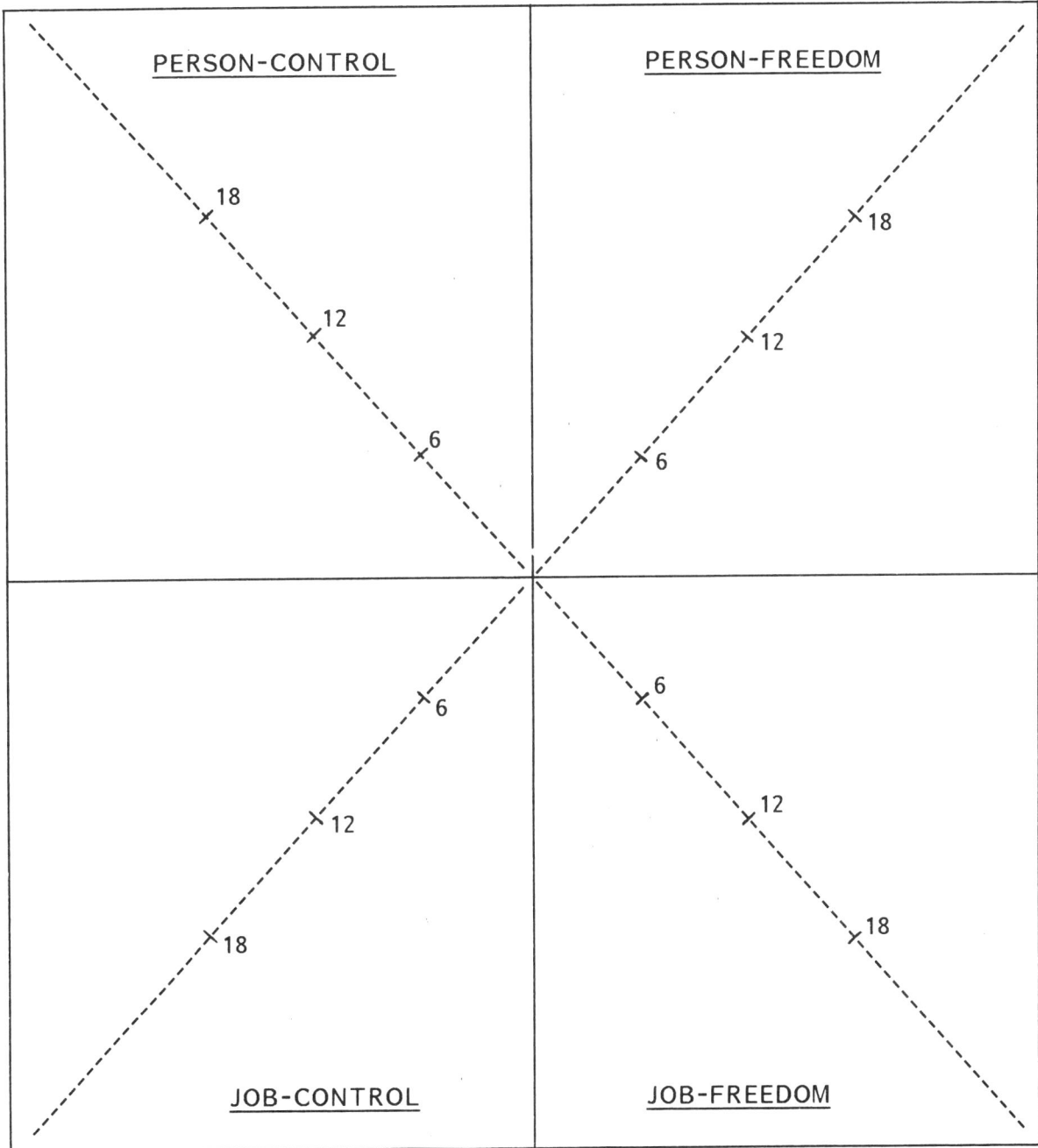

HANDOUT READING ON SCHOOL CULTURE

Profiling organisations: The SIGMA[1] system for mapping organisational elements

The purpose of this instrument is to map out some very important parameters of organisations and to enable one to conceptualise, design or develop organisations which reflect a particular set of values and which are appropriate to the age of rapid change in which we live. The framework first appeared in its trial form as an instrument for a 'Survey of Work Life Preferences' produced for the National Institute for Development of Educational Administrators (IDEA) of the Ministry of Education, Bangkok, Thailand.

It must be emphasised that organisations are not seen as being 'real' in any sense of objective reality. Rather they are seen as existing mainly as subjective constructs in the minds of those who experience them. In carrying out an analysis using this method, therefore, it is essential to tap into the perceptions of a cross-section of organisational members at least rather than rely on the perceptions of one person or work group. This essentially phenomenological approach to organisations, its rationale and methodology, are explored in Elliott-Kemp and Williams (1985).

The conceptual framework for the system is built around two fundamental polarities in organisational design and development:

● the balance or imbalance between freedom and control: a polarity which tends to reflect the prime issue in organisational behaviour,

● the amount of emphasis on the person as a unique individual as distinct from an emphasis on the job or role that the individual performs.

From these two key issues a pair of intersecting polarities is created, thus enabling one to anlayse organisations in terms of four 'elements' falling between the points of intersection of the polarities (Figure 1).

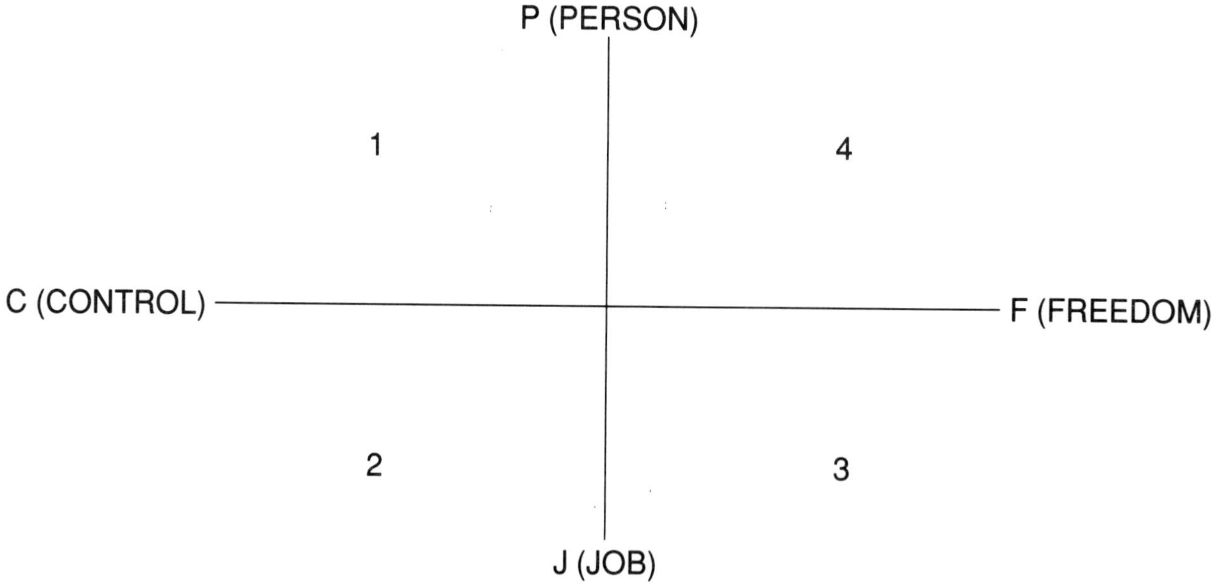

Figure 1 The conceptual framework

All organisations can be seen as consisting of a distinctive blend of these four basic elements in the model:

1. PC – autocratic
2. JC – bureaucratic
3. JF – temporary systems, or 'adhocratic'

4. PF – networks ('reticulocratic').

The key identifying characteristic or 'indicator' in each element is found in the fusion of the two polarities which define its boundaries in the model: thus networks (element 4) are characterised by the degree of personal freedom, and the essence of the bureaucratic element (2) is the exercise of control by means of a carefully defined job or role (Figure 2).

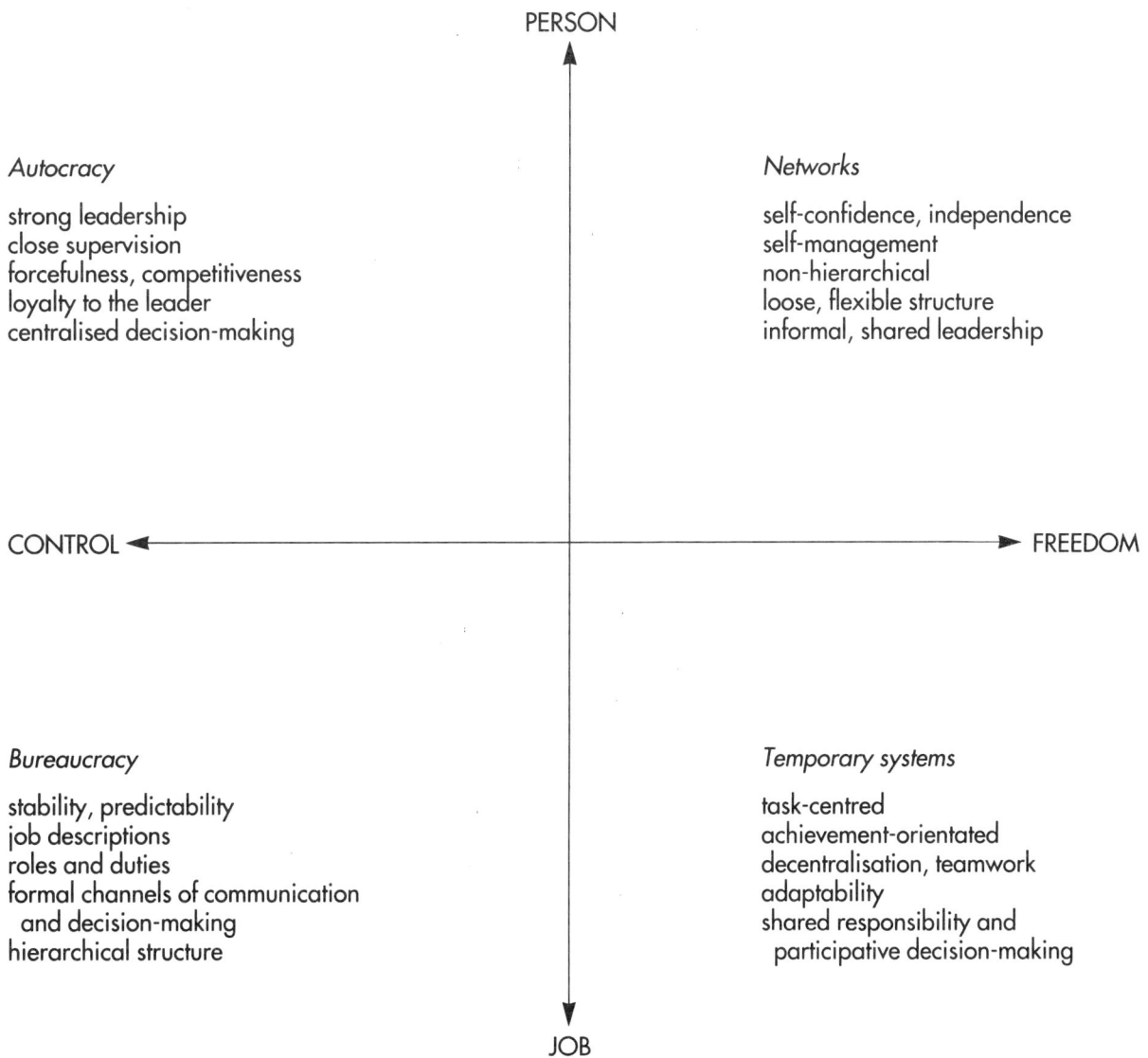

PERSON

Autocracy

strong leadership
close supervision
forcefulness, competitiveness
loyalty to the leader
centralised decision-making

Networks

self-confidence, independence
self-management
non-hierarchical
loose, flexible structure
informal, shared leadership

CONTROL ◄─────────────────────────► FREEDOM

Bureaucracy

stability, predictability
job descriptions
roles and duties
formal channels of communication
  and decision-making
hierarchical structure

Temporary systems

task-centred
achievement-orientated
decentralisation, teamwork
adaptability
shared responsibility and
  participative decision-making

JOB

Figure 2
*Characteristic aspects or qualities emphasised
in each of the four elements*

Traditionally, most organisations have relied heavily on the elements on the left side of the model, sometimes with only a minimal acknowledgement of the right side. Indeed it has often been the fate of elements 3 and 4 (JF, PF) to exist only in the shape of the informal organisation – the 'underground' or 'grapevine' – not officially recognised where the bureaucratic element is predominating and often under direct attack or manipulation from above in organisations which are primarily autocratic.

A traditional organisational profile would typically resemble Figure 3, where a bureaucratic structure appears to be struggling to limit the autocratic leader:

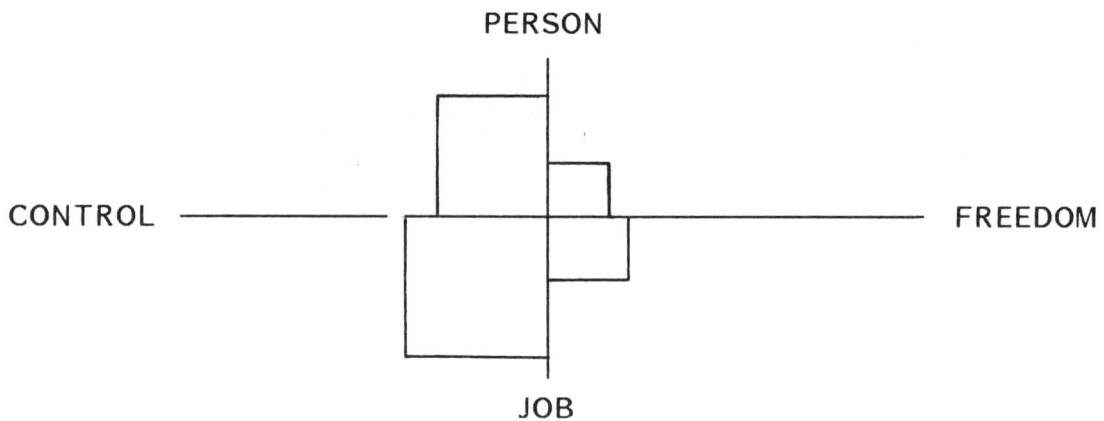

Figure 3

It is possible to make a case for the relative dominance of one specific element under certain circumstances. The autocratic (PC) element will be most appropriate in times of crisis, where decisiveness and rapid implementation of decisions are required, or where staff are deficient in experience, expertise or commitment. But at its worst it may result in unbridled favouritism and paternalism, and capricious leadership based on personal whim or mood. The autocratic leader may create dependency among colleagues rather than developing their potential. The worst of such leaders may perceive the organisation and its resources mainly as an aid to gratifying their personal wants; as a kind of personal playground.

The bureaucratic element (JC) at its best can act as an antidote to the unbridled excesses of the autocrat. It is a social invention which uses reason, rules, structure and predictability in the design of organisations, and historically much of our civilisation has relied on this element. But at its worst bureaucracy is rigid, inert and unresponsive. It is extremely difficult to modify, where a rapidly changing environment requires a matching response from the organisation. At the very heart of the bureaucratic element lies an impersonality, even a robot syndrome, where people are perceived primarily as roles, categories or functions rather than unique and complex individuals. The dominance of the bureaucratic JC element in an age of rapid change means that procedures and policy which no longer serve any useful purpose will still continue to be adhered to because there is no facility for adaptation or self-renewal: the dominance of the JC element determines that the organisation will navigate through the rear-view mirror, forever looking back to the past, instead of through the windscreen. Bureaucracy thus continues to try to solve yesterday's problems rather than the problems of today and tomorrow.

The turning point: the coming of the information society

The traditional methods for designing, structuring and managing organisations are derived from the age of manufacturing industry and the public utilities of an age of relative stability. They are no longer appropriate for the new era into which we are already moving – the age of information. The information society is characterised by an environment of rapid, turbulent change, with a correspondingly rapid development of new technology. The new information society will depend primarily not on land, capital or raw materials as in the traditional economies of the previous agricultural and industrial revolutions, but on investment in human capital (Drucker, 1970; Naisbitt and Abudene 1986, Stonier, 1983). The strategic resource of the post-industrial society is information, and the key worker is the professional 'knowledge worker' whose prime task is the creation, processing, evaluation and dissemination of information.

The highly educated and highly skilled knowledge worker will not be prepared to become an anonymous cog in a bureaucratic machine or a helpless pawn in the hands of a paternalistic or autocratic leader, however benevolent that leader may be. The professional knowledge worker seeks autonomy, challenge and professional growth and is not prepared to tolerate the inertia, frustration and dehumanising effects of so many of the traditional organisational patterns. The SIGMA-type organisation (JF or PF dominant) is genuinely educational or developmental in its rationale, processes and results. It is 'empowering' and 'enabling' in its effects, where autocracy and bureaucracy are ultimately disabling and de-powering.

It is important to realise, however, that one can never completely eliminate the PC and JC elements in organisations. Bureaucratic behaviour will be necessary in establishing routines, recording systems and regulations, all of which have a place in organisation development, especially in the setting up of a new school or classroom. Autocratic or paternalistic leadership and decision-making comes into its own when an organisation faces a crisis, or when staff lack appropriate knowledge, skill or experience. The issue is not whether we have a particular element in an organisation or not, for all four are necessary. It is the appropriateness of the 'mix' of these elements to the situation that one must examine (Handy, 1986).

The most appropriate organisational profile for the information society would consequently appear to be like the one depicted in Figure 4:

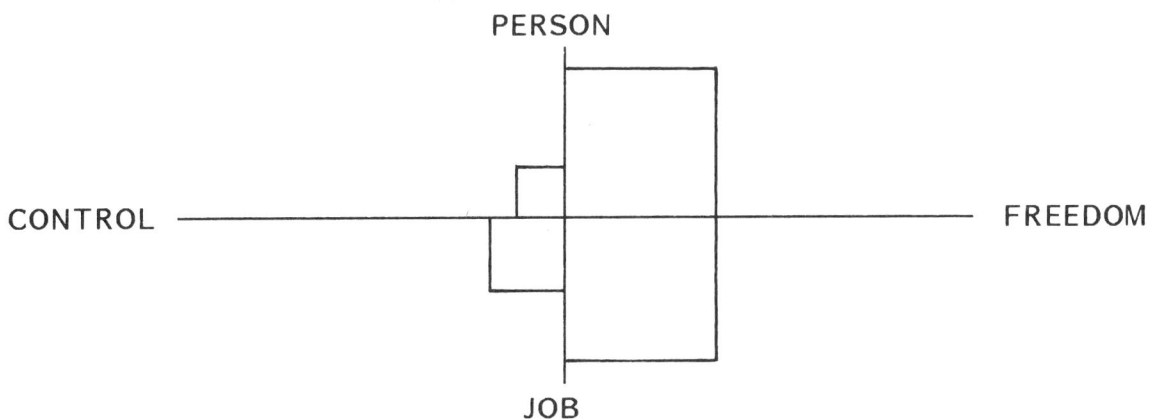

PERSON

CONTROL ——————————— FREEDOM

JOB

Figure 4

The members of this kind of organisation would be highly trained and educated and very adaptable in their response to needs, problems and tasks. They would not be ensnared in the 'primadonna' trap (the desire to work in isolation from colleagues) but would be members of a team, helping and reinforcing each other. They would be confident and committed, and would expect as a right the shared responsibility and participative decision-making for a professional among fellow-professionals. They would above all else be self-renewing, and their synergy would consequently help create a self-renewing organisation.

Note
[1]SIGMA is an acronym representing a set of particular values and assumptions which stem from a humanistic philosophy. The individual letters of the acronym 'SIGMA' stand for 'Self-Initiated Group Managed Action' and the emphasis in a SIGMA organisation is on the creation of a shared purpose and vision through self-help, mutual support and flexible, highly adaptive structures. This material for diagnosis and development of a school's culture is an abbreviated version of SIGMA TWO (Culture), published by PAVIC Publications, Sheffield City Polytechnic (UK). The complete system and manual are available from the polytechnic.

References and bibliography

BOISOT, M. (1987) *Information and Organisations: The Manager as Anthropologist*, Fontana-Collins.

DEAL, T.E. and KENNEDY, A.A. (1982) *Corporate Cultures – The Rites and Rituals of Corporate Life*, Addison-Wesley.

DRUCKER, P. (1970) *Technology, Management and Society*, Pan Management Books.

ELLIOTT-KEMP, J. and WILLIAMS, G.L. (1985) 'Towards a Reconciliation of Systems Theory and Existentialism', in SHARMA, M. (ed.) *The Systems Approach*, Himalaya Publishing House, India, New Delhi.

ELLIOTT-KEMP, J. (1989) SIGMA Two, *Improving the Culture of your Organisation*, PAVIC Publications, Sheffield City Polytechnic.

HANDY, C. (1986) *Gods of Management*, rev. edn, Souvenir Press.

HARRISON, R. (1972) 'How to Describe your Organisation', *Harvard Business Review*, Sept-Oct.

NAISBITT, J. and ABUDENE, P. (1986) *Re-inventing the Corporation*, Futura-Macdonald.

PETERS, T. and WATERMAN, R. (1982) *In Search of Excellence*, Harper & Row.

STONIER T. (1983) *The Wealth of Information: a profile of the post-industrial economy*, Methuen.

An inventory for school-based review and development

This inventory for school-based review and development draws on contemporary literature on the effective school or college and our own experience as teachers, heads and in-service trainers and consultants.

The 1980s saw a remarkable growth of research and its application to school development. One of the most wide-ranging studies has been the OECD International Schools Improvement Project (ISIP), based on work in ten countries. This project has generated a range of publications, some intended for researchers, academics or policy-makers, and others whose intended audience is practitioners engaged in school-based review. Among the most useful of these ISIP publications are Bollen and Hopkins (1987), Miles *et al* (1987) and Hopkins (1988). This last work examines different school review systems from around the world which provide diagnostic instruments and resource materials for school review. One of the resources featured in this guide is the SIGMA project, published by Sheffield City Polytechnic, UK.

SIGMA (Self-Initiated Group Managed Action) is a school development project which provides comprehensive resource materials and INSET training for schools and colleges, including development workshops for head-teachers, middle management, work teams and whole school staff groups. The SIGMA project INSET training has been used in a variety of different schools and countries worldwide and the inventory for school-based review which is presented here was originally piloted as part of the SIGMA resource bank. We are grateful to PAVIC Publications, of Sheffield City Polytechnic, for permission to publish it here.

The inventory

The inventory is not intended to be a self-contained or closed-ended resource for long-term school review and development. It is envisaged that as a school staff gain experience in carrying out school-based review they will make their own additions and amendments to the instrument in the light of emerging needs and problems. We regard the **process** of doing school-based review as perhaps its most important aspect and would wish to emphasise its organic nature. Though we believe in the importance of establishing a clear structure to begin with, we do not believe this should become a mechanical formula or dogma.

Staff should therefore be actively encouraged to improve the inventory after a year's trial. In this way it will become *their* inventory. An increased sense of ownership will tend to result in increased levels of commitment to school development.

The material which follows consists of the review instrument itself and a section on the process of using and following up the diagnostic phase.

The major themes of the review are:

1. The guiding value system of the school.
2. Quality of work life: meaning, motivation, leadership and rewards.
3. Staff development; teamwork, meetings, stress management and support networks.
4. Administrative structure: organisation, rules and regulations, timetabling, records, paperwork and student supervision.
5. Role clarity, responsibilities and performance.
6. Environmental stance: community support and relationships with parents and governors.
7. Creativity, innovation and the management of change.

Introducing the school-based review inventory

When using the review system, the first decision to make is which of the major areas to select for review and development. The method recommended for identifying the institution's priority area is to ballot the whole staff group. This should be preceded by a short briefing session on the purpose and rationale of the review and the content areas of the inventory. Staff involvement in this decision will help to ensure ownership of the project by those who will ultimately need to act upon the findings of the review process. The aim is to foster a climate in which staff see themslves as active agents of purposeful and worthwhile change and development rather than passive recipients of change implemented or decided by others.

Each of the major review areas can provide ideas to work on for a whole term, and sometimes an entire year. It is not normally recommended that schools try to work concurrently on more than one major section.

The biggest constraint on doing school-based review and development is usually a lack of easily identified 'slack' time in which to carry it out. The initial stage of a development project requires a clear day for staff to work together. After the first diagnostic review and analysis of data, the planning and monitoring can be managed by task groups who will need time allocated to meetings. Continuing evaluation and planning will be best formalised by a half-day in which all staff can meet again, about four to six weeks after the initial review day.

There are obvious implications in taking on school-based review to identify the whole of an institution's INSET needs and priorities. It is essential to map out all needs and plans in a coherent statement, schedule or flow chart. Change is more likely to be effective where the development plan is fully familiar to staff and governors. Staff will have little or no confidence in a development policy or INSET planning which appears to be haphazard or piecemeal.

The major priority areas of the SIGMA school-based review inventory

Priority Rating → High

1. The guiding value system (looking at the values which underpin work life).

2. Quality of work life: meaning, motivation, leadership and rewards.

3. Staff development (including teamwork, meetings, stress mangement and support networks).

4. Administrative structure (including organisation, rules and regulations, timetabling, records, paperwork and student supervision).

5. Role clarity, role negotiation and accountability (including roles, responsibilities and performance).

6. Environmental stance: community support and relationships with parents and governors.

7. Creativity, innovation and the management of change.

The guiding value system

In this section the scoring system differs from that used in the other major sections.

You are asked, in assessing the guiding value system, to enter two scores, each with a cross (x):

I (Ideal) – where you would wish the school to be *ideally*, in relation to the emphasis placed on this value.

A (Actual) – the amount of emphasis we seem to place on this value now.

Note – You are asked to respond not just to the amount of talk about guiding values but to the extent to which the school actually *models* or *exemplifies* the values in staff behaviour and day-to-day life in the school.

SIGMA School-Based Review
Section 1

THE GUIDING VALUE SYSTEM

1. We regard interpersonal or social skills as important to both staff and students.

	Low			High
Ideal				
Actual				

2. We believe that people should learn to appreciate what others are feeling and have consideration for their feelings.

	Low			High
Ideal				
Actual				

3. Our students need to appreciate the unique contribution each subject makes to our civilisation through its key concepts and methods of problem-solving.

	Low			High
Ideal				
Actual				

4. It is important that students learn to conform and to be obedient: the world of work will require this of them.

	Low			High
Ideal				
Actual				

5. The most important thing our students should gain from the curriculum is 'learning how to learn' so that they can stand on their own feet.

	Low			High
Ideal				
Actual				

6. Students must learn to be responsible people and therefore must play a part in being responsible for their own learning and their learning environment.

	Low			High
Ideal				
Actual				

7. We make effective use of assemblies, ceremonies and displays to communicate our school's culture and values.

	Low			High
Ideal				
Actual				

8. We are able to criticise ourselves and accept criticism from others in a positive way without being defensive or aggressive.

	Low			High
Ideal				
Actual				

9. We regard our work as a source of personal fulfilment.

	Low			High
Ideal				
Actual				

10. Staff involvement in curriculum development and decision-making is taken seriously.

	Low			High
Ideal				
Actual				

11. 'Skill', 'quality' and 'expertise' are high on our list of professional concerns.

	Low			High
Ideal				
Actual				

12. Staff are consulted on issues which concern or affect them.

	Low			High
Ideal				
Actual				

13. Colleagues have trust in each other.

	Low			High
Ideal				
Actual				

14. Staff trust their leaders and vice versa.

	Low			High
Ideal				
Actual				

15. Leaders are accessible and approachable.

	Low			High
Ideal				
Actual				

16. No-one has to work in isolation: there is support or help readily available.

	Low			High
Ideal				
Actual				

17. We have a clear sense of identity as a school, and reinforce this both through the things we do within the school and in our stance to the world outside.

	Low			High
Ideal				
Actual				

18. We know and value the things we do especially well which help to give the school its unique qualities.

	Low			High
Ideal				
Actual				

19. The concept of 'quality control' is taken seriously and involves everyone.

	Low			High
Ideal				
Actual				

20. People get recognition or appreciation for a job or task well done.

	Low			High
Ideal				
Actual				

21. We actively listen to what our students and parents say about our school.

	Low			High
Ideal				
Actual				

22. We take pride in being a friendly organisation.

	Low			High
Ideal				
Actual				

23. The staff are our most valuable resource and we reflect this feeling in our respect for each other's expertise.

	Low			High
Ideal				
Actual				

24. We appreciate and strive for consensus in the way we work as a staff.

	Low			High
Ideal				
Actual				

25. We support a competitive ethic: competition helps to create or maintain high standards.

	Low			High
Ideal				
Actual				

26. We attach a high value to teamwork: it is more important to learn collaboration than competition. People show that they value each other by helping each other.

	Low			High
Ideal				
Actual				

27. Open communication is vital: effectiveness always relies on honest feedback.

	Low			High
Ideal				
Actual				

28. Personal autonomy is important in our work.

	Low			High
Ideal				
Actual				

29. It is important to present a solid front: we must be seen to have staff unanimity on all major issues.

	Low			High
Ideal				
Actual				

30. We value efficiency: it is important to be well organised and not to waste our resources.

	Low			High
Ideal				
Actual				

31. We genuinely respect the individual and have concern for individual well-being.

	Low			High
Ideal				
Actual				

32. We value training and development and try to ensure that everyone has both opportunities and responsibilities for personal and professional growth.

	Low			High
Ideal				
Actual				

SIGMA school-based review

Scoring instructions for Sections 2-7

Each statement in Sections 2-7 of this review instrument is accompanied by a space in which to record your view by placing a cross (x) in the appropriate box:

Low score   High score

1	2	3	4

Key: Score 4   Statement is true. This is one of our strengths.
                Score 3   Quite satisfactory.
                Score 2   Barely adequate in this area.
                Score 1   I believe this is one of our problem areas.

Please do not discuss your responses at this stage. There will be opportunities to share our perceptions when everyone has completed the scoring system and results are examined together.

SIGMA School-Based Review
Section 2

QUALITY OF WORK, LIFE: MEANING, MOTIVATION, LEADERSHIP AND REWARDS

1. I feel good about my work more often than I feel bad.

Low   High

2. I believe my contribution to the school makes a difference.

Low   High

3. I am aware of how my work fits in and contributes to the system of the whole school.

Low   High

4. Staff commitment to the values and goals of the school is high.

Low   High

5. Staff efforts and achievements are high.

Low   High

6. My work is challenging in a positive way.

Low   High

7. My contribution is valued by my students.

Low   High

8. My contribution is valued by colleagues and leaders.

Low   High

9. I feel my work is appreciated by parents and governors.

Low   High

10. I have the sense of belonging to a team and have opportunities to help and be helped by other colleagues.

Low   High

11. There are opportunities available to influence others, including the chance to participate in decision-making and influence organisational policy.

Low   High

12. Leaders will listen to my views even though they may not agree with them.

Low   High

13. I have some areas of my work where I can be creative and free to do things in my own way.

Low   High

14. I can develop new expertise and useful skills in my work here.

Low   High

15. We have a high level of trust and support among immediate colleagues.

Low   High

16. Mutual trust and support between school leaders and staff is high.

Low   High

17. Leaders set good examples to others in their behaviour.

Low   High

18. Staff feel confident in their leaders' ability to manage.

Low   High

19. Staff are aware of the tasks and functions that school leaders perform and how these are fitted into the leader's day-to-day work.

Low   High

20. Leaders at all levels in the school are aware of the workload carried by their staff and the pressures and problems they cope with.

Low   High

STAFF DEVELOPMENT, TEAMWORK, SUPPORT NETWORKS AND MEETINGS

1. We have structures for identification and negotiation of development needs at different levels within the school.

Low   High

2. Individual needs are taken into account.

Low   High

3. We consider the development needs of departmental and year teams.

Low   High

4. Organisational needs such as management training for leaders at different levels are adequately catered for.

Low   High

5. There are low levels of coercion or perceived threat in development policy. Staff do not feel that they are manipulated from above.

Low   High

6. We ensure that needs identification for staff development is followed by appropriate INSET.

Low   High

7. We have a coherent INSET policy.

Low   High

8. Staff accept ownership of their INSET policy and practices because they have been involved in policy fomulation.

Low   High

9. Review and appraisal are accepted in a positive way as an integral part of the development process.

Low   High

10. I feel I am stretched and challenged by the demands of my job rather than threatened or harmed.

Low   High

11. We are sensitive to stressed or anxious colleagues.

Low   High

12. Support networks exist at all levels to help people cope with stress and anxiety.

Low   High

13. Staff feel able and willing to discuss their sources of stress with chosen colleagues.

Low   High

14. Staff try to avoid working in isolation from each other.

Low   High

15. Staff are involved with each other and committed to teamwork.

Low   High

16. We believe in a collaborative ethic rather than thriving on interpersonal or intergroup competition.

Low   High

17. Individuality is enhanced, not diminished, by membership of a team.

Low   High

18. Whenever we have meetings their rationale is always made clear to participants.

Low   High

19. We make sure that the size of a group is appropriate to the purpose of a meeting (eg large numbers for giving information, small numbers for discussion).

Low   High

20. Adequate time is allocated for achieving the goals of a meeting.

Low   High

21. Staff have a 'model' or evaluative system with which to assess behaviour, processes and outcomes of meetings.

Low   High

22. This evaluative system is applied to meetings in order to plan and monitor progress.

Low   High

23. Meetings usually achieve the stated goals.

Low   High

ADMINISTRATIVE STRUCTURE

1. The school is well organised, and this helps staff and students to feel secure.

Low   High

2. Existing paperwork is necessary and does not get in the way of more important things.

Low   High

3. Existing rules and regulations are clear and necessary.

Low   High

4. Rules and regulations are enforced.

Low   High

5. The timetable is fair.

Low   High

6. The timetable runs smoothly.

Low   High

7. Student profiles or records are accurate and up-to-date.

Low   High

8. Record-keeping is not too heavy a burden.

Low   High

9. Records are valued sources of information.

Low				High

10. The system of duty rosters is fair.

Low				High

11. There is adequate supervision of students at all times.

Low				High

12. Student attendance is monitored effectively.

Low				High

13. The school is prompt and efficient in following up absences.

Low				High

14. The amount of unjustified absences is low.

Low				High

15. Students know that if they are absent they will be missed and the school will take action.

Low				High

ROLE CLARITY, ROLE NEGOTIATION AND ACCOUNTABILITY

1. Staff avoid working in isolation from each other.

Low			High

2. I am clear about my own role and responsibilities.

Low			High

3. I am clear about the roles and responsibilities of colleagues in my immediate role set (ie in my department or year group).

Low			High

4. I am clear about the role and responsibilities of my immediate superior or team leader.

Low			High

5. My immediate colleagues seem to have a clear understanding of my role and responsibilities.

Low			High

6. I am happy with the allocation of roles and responsibilities within my year team, department or role set.

Low			High

7. Colleagues fulfil their roles and responsibilities effectively.

Low			High

8. We have the confidence, skill and mutual trust required to re-negotiate any aspects of a role with each other.

Low			High

9. We understand and accept reciprocal accountability, where we are accountable to each other and where effectiveness depends on roles which complement each other.

Low   High

10. We are able to discuss mutual role performance honestly, with low feelings of threat to self and others.

Low   High

11. We have a built-in system of accountability in the sense that we 'give an account of' our purposes, methods and achievements to each other as an ongoing part of our work.

Low   High

12. This information is collated and summarised and made available for headteachers, governors and inspectors.

Low   High

ENVIRONMENTAL STANCE

1. The school is aware of the needs, circumstances and aspirations of its parents and makes use of this information.

Low — High

2. We have structures to involve parents in supporting and monitoring their children's learning.

Low — High

3. There is an ongoing dialogue on children's learning between parents and school; any problems are resolved in a climate of mutual respect.

Low — High

4. We are developing ways of using parents as a curriculum resource.

Low — High

5. All parents, irrespective of social, economic or ethnic group, are valued and listened to. Parental involvment is sought sympathetically from all parents.

Low — High

6. We are working to involve all parents in the process of institutional review and development.

Low — High

7. The school curriculum demonstrates an awareness of the needs, aspirations and histories of the communities it serves.

Low — High

8. Individuals, groups and institutions in our local communities are used as resources for learning.

Low — High

9. Community groups are invited to use the school as a resource.

Low   High

10. All sections of our community are kept informed as to our aims, and the achievements of our students.

Low   High

11. We are aware of community perceptions of our institution and use this knowledge in the process of review and development.

Low   High

12. Governors are given structured induction on the aims and systems of our school.

Low   High

13. Governors receive continuous and accessible information on student achievements and institutional developments.

Low   High

14. Governors' training is seen as a school responsibility as well as a function of the Education Authority.

Low   High

15. We are developing a system to link governors, parents and school in a network of mutual support.

Low   High

16. Governors are actively involved in the processes of school review and development.

Low   High

CREATIVITY, INNOVATION AND THE MANAGEMENT OF CHANGE

1. We keep in touch with the ways in which colleagues in other schools are trying out new ideas.

Low			High

2. We are open-minded about new ideas and practices.

Low			High

3. Staff are willing to challenge assumptions which underpin existing structures and practices rather than perpetuate systems no longer useful or relevant.

Low			High

4. We deliberately seek and try out new ways of doing things.

Low			High

5. There is willingness on the part of staff to evaluate our purposes, as well as processes and results.

Low			High

6. We are able to admit our mistakes in innovation.

Low			High

7. We are able to learn from our mistakes.

Low			High

8. Creative conflict of ideas is encouraged and seldom degenerates to the level of interpersonal conflict.

Low			High

9. All staff are involved at some time or other in the sensing of needs and potential problems.

Low   High

10. We have effective and efficient communication channels and co-ordinating structures to help action on needs or problems when identified.

Low   High

11. We have the capability to manage innovation well in the following areas:
    - careful and thorough planning of change,

Low   High

    - involvement or consultation with those carrying out the change,

Low   High

    - appropriate training of staff,

Low   High

    - realistic time scale for preparation and implementation,

Low   High

    - monitoring systems which provide feedback on what is happening during the process of change,

Low   High

    - adequate provision of resources for the innovation.

Low   High

12. We are willing to try experimental or pilot projects to assess their worth or feasibility.

Low | | | | High

13. We ensure that new ideas of proved worth are fully incorporated into the fabric of the school so that they can be absorbed by all.

Low | | | | High

14. Succession planning is well managed. Key innovators ensure they have prepared colleagues so that changes do not collapse or wither away when the original innovators leave.

Low | | | | High

15. There is concern for value or quality in innovation rather than novelty for its own sake or as a status symbol.

Low | | | | High

16. Concern for value or quality underpins the justification for systems or practices which remain unchanged.

Low | | | | High

17. Staff are aware of what is happening in different parts of the system through effective communication channels, both formal and informal (eg personal networks and the 'grapevine').

Low | | | | High

18. When multiple pressures for change come from outside the school we are able to fix priorities and manage changes in a coherent and rational way without betraying our values and standards.

Low | | | | High

19. Leaders in the school inform and protect staff facing rapid and turbulent change by communicating a coherent view, or 'mental map', of coming changes which can help people to put them in perspective.

Low | | | | High

MANAGING THE PROCESS OF SCHOOL-BASED REVIEW AND DEVELOPMENT

This section provides suggestions and checklists for those who are responsible for managing or facilitating the development process.

Having an instrument for school review is only the starting point. The instrument is simply a tool – it is the skill and sensitivity with which the instrument is used, together with the thinking and planning of how identified needs are to be dealt with, which will determine the success of a development project.

Data collection and analysis

When staff have completed their individual responses to the inventory it will be necessary to collect and process data. The evidence from learning theory strongly suggests that the more immediate the feedback the more effective is the learning. The simplest method of data collection is by means of blank grids on OHP transparencies or flip charts (Figure 3.2).

Area for Review: Statement Number		ROLE CLARITY Total Scores		
	Needs 1	2	3	Strengths 4
1				
2				
3				
4 etc.				

Figure 3.2

Staff are asked to assemble in work groups/teams and respond to each item by a show of hands according to where they have marked their score sheet on each statement. The totals are entered on the grid by group leaders or facilitators.

When this has been completed it is important to highlight the strengths first (ie large scores in columns 3 and 4). Staff can then examine the biggest scores which fall in column 1 or 2. Each group should first be encouraged to explore the precise meaning of their scores in column 1 and then move on to positive action for improvement.

The group leader should ask members to focus on the following two issues in their discussion:

1. What precisely do we need to do in order to make things better? (ie specific actions)
2. What are the things we must avoid doing if we are to improve the situation?

The facilitator should list group decisions about these 'do's and don'ts' on a flip chart for all to see. When this has been done to everyone's satisfaction the leader should introduce the idea of written 'commitments' or 'contracts'.

Negotiating agreement contracts

We must acknowledge that we are all fallible. Resolutions and promises may be made with great enthusiasm and complete sincerity, but the passage of time and the multiple pressures and demands of the everyday and the commonplace will ensure that, for most of us, the commitment to change will wane. This can happen with all kinds of intentions to change – from New Year Resolutions to major innovations or development projects.

One way to help people to keep to their resolutions to change is to agree a written commitment or 'contract', to run for an agreed period of time. This contract would be negotiated within a group or team of people who would, themselves, have the power to carry out the necessary action(s) and to monitor progress towards achieving the goals of the agreement.

The form of such a written commitment should, ideally, include:

- the specific area of concern arising from the diagnostic exercise, including the goal(s) to be achieved,
- the dates of the initial commitment and monitoring (formative review),
- agreed action on the part of group members. This should include specific positive and negative 'indicators', ie things we *will do* and things we will *avoid*,
- notes on progress, including problems arising,
- the signatures of all members of the group. This has an important symbolic value in affirming a commitment to effect change.

The fully completed 'commitment sheets' would subsequently provide information for a summative review with colleagues at the end of the agreed period. The written material would finally be valuable as the basis for a school development report for governors or inspectors.

An example of such a 'commitment sheet' to be completed by group members can be found below.

SCHOOL-BASED REVIEW

Reciprocal Agreement   Date ....

Relevant inventory issue(s)

AGREED ACTION	Monitoring Notes	Date
Specific things we will do:		
1.		
2.		
3.		
4.		
5.		
Specific things we will try to avoid doing:		
1.		
2.		
3.		
4.		
5.		

Signatures:

Group, team or department:

School-based review: a checklist of key stages for group leaders or facilitators

1. Decide when time is ripe to do review.
2. Create appropriate blocks of available time to do review and development: one day for initial review exercise plus times for following up matters arising from this.
3. Explain rationale and assumptions to staff. Allow sufficient time to answer any questions.
4. Present overview of the system, including a brief summary of the seven key focus areas covered by the instrument.
   Allow time to answer any questions.
5. Select the focus area for review from the seven key areas.
6. Carry out the diagnosis, leading to identification of development needs within the chosen area.
7. Form task groups based on work relationships.
8. Reinforce areas of strength. (This 'celebration' of the positive feedback should on no account be omitted – reviewing is not just identifying negative aspects.)
9. Decide priority areas to work on.
10. Explore personal meanings of responses to key statements.
11. Identify objectives, involving everyone concerned, and negotiate 'contracts'.
    Agree time scale and monitoring systems.
12. Keep all staff informed about what groups have decided. (Allocate special notice boards for this, uncluttered by administrative or other paper.)
13. Implement agreed plans.
14. Monitor and feed back progress.
15. Publicise information on progress, keeping all staff informed.
16. Ensure that staff receive recognition and appreciation of their effort and commitment.
17. Evaluate at end of agreed period and decide on next stage as appropriate.
18. Provide staff forum for exchanging experiences and ideas, especially networks which cut across normal work groups.

References

BOLLEN, R. and HOPKINS, D. (1987) *School-Based Review: Towards a Praxis* Acco Leuven (Belgium) for OECD.

HOPKINS, D. (1988) *Doing School-Based Review: Instruments and Guidelines*, Acco Leuven (Belgium) for OECD.

MILES, M.B., EKHOLM, M and VANDENBERGHE (eds) (1987) *Lasting School Improvement: Exploring the Process of Institutionalisation*, Acco Leuven (Belgium) for OECD.

The innovation or change

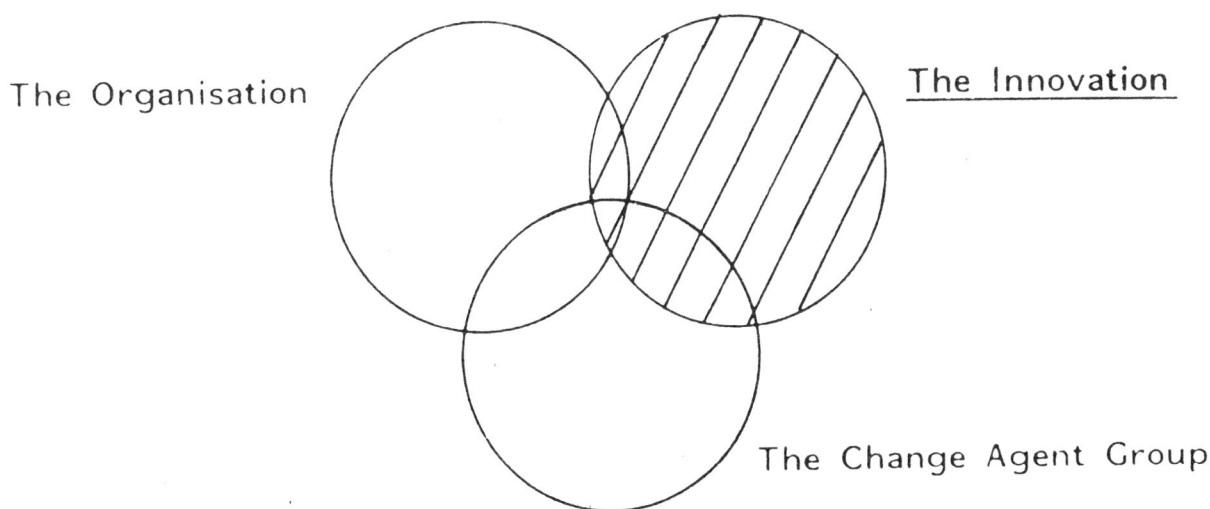

The Organisation   The Innovation

The Change Agent Group

Figure 4.1

Analysing the innovation,
> – its purpose and value
> – costs and implications.

Staff perceptions of innovation,
> – the EPIC questionnaire.

Conclusions and decisions,
> – making judgments based on the analysis,
> – alternative approaches to introducing change.

An innovation checklist,
> – a collection of reminders for change agents.

The innovation

In this chapter we shall focus on issues pertaining to the innovation or change itself and its implications for the school. An inventory of questions is presented, covering different aspects which may need to be addressed before the decision to implement the change is made.

In terms of the whole process of managing innovation and change we may picture this stage in the cycle, as in Figure 4.2.

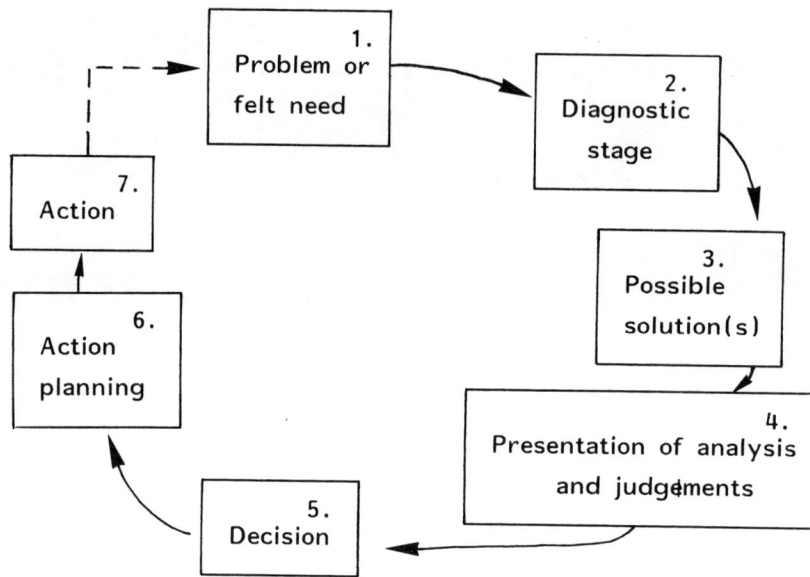

Figure 4.2

Let us suppose that one of the areas in the school-based review has been selected by the school (felt need) and as a result of their responses to the questionnaire (diagnostic stage) it seems that major changes in this area are needed (possible solution).

This chapter provides materials to assist the school in the succeeding stages of the process:

- analysing a proposed change, its purpose, benefits, costs and implications for all concerned,
- making the final decision about the proposed change, including how it should be introduced into the school,
- producing relevant information about the change for those with legitimate interests (eg staff, governors, parents, students). The analysis could form the basis of a report.
- planning to implement the change, if it is deemed useful, acceptable and workable.

The cyclical model is, of course, an ideal model. The process of managing change is seldom a simple linear flow and in real life the action may jump forwards and backwards in terms of this 'rational' process. This does not invalidate the model – we need a mental picture of what the process should, ideally, look like as a 'mindhold' to make our thoughts and actions as rational as possible, even though the real world will never conform to a purely rational or logical pattern. (Any teacher will appreciate this in relation to lesson planning, teaching and classroom management.)

The inventory for innovation analysis is succeeded by an exercise to explore staff reactions to an innovation, especially their perceptions of its possible consequences for them and how they feel about these. (EPIC).

Following this is a summary section which poses some questions about the change agents' conclusions from completing the previous sections, together with a review of some of the major decision choices available to the change agent team.

The last section in this work is an innovation checklist – a set of reminders for a change agent team, especially those who have leadership or mangement responsibilities. This consists of reminders about the important things which should be done *before* a major change is introduced.

Analysing a projected innovation or change

This innovation analysis document contains an inventory of questions designed to be used as worksheets for those proposing a significant change.

When used in conjunction with the EPIC questionnaire (Exploring Personal Implications of Change) it will provide data to assist in decision-making about the adoption, postponement or rejection of a proposed change.

Preliminary information

What is the nature and purpose of the change?

What is the background and need for this change? (What need will it fulfil? What problems will it solve?)

Are the purposes and nature of the change acceptable and easily understood by relevant groups of users or clients?
- the school staff?
- the pupils?
- the parents?
- school governors?

How do you know?

Values

What values does the innovation support or embody? (Note both explicit and implicit values.)

What values, by implication, does the innovation appear to ignore or reject?

In what ways do the content and spirit of the innovation appear to be influenced by, or fit, theories or assumptions relating to:
- human nature?
- human learning, development and potential?

Outcomes

What are the intended outcomes as a result of adopting this innovation?

What will be the immediate benefits? (Who will benefit and how?)
What will be the longer-term benefits?

Can you identify any possible unintended outcomes? What 'knock-on' effects may be expected? (eg on school roles and structure, timetable, staff grouping and relationships, use of space)
Can you identify which of these unintended outcomes and 'knock-on' effects are likely to be harmful and which beneficial? (Give reasons for this.)

Implications and costs

Financial, staffing and other resource implications
What will be the initial setting-up costs for equipment, materials or services? (Give details.)

What will be the recurring costs of maintaining or replacing materials, equipment and any other resources?

Which members of staff will be involved?

What changes in their role are implied by the adoption of the innovation?

What changes in work groups will be implied?

How does the innovation relate to what has been done previously? (ie Is it a continuity or discontinuity?)

What is your estimate of the amount of time necessary *before* implementation for familiarisation and training activities?

How will these be provided? Who will be responsible, and when will these activities occur?

What additional demands will be placed on staff as a result of the change? (Initially, and in the long term.)

What implications are there for students or pupils? (eg with reference to teaching – learning methods, subject choice, patterns of organisation, assessment or relationships.)

What major problems can be envisaged arising from implementation of the innovation in *non-ideal* situations? (eg with inexperienced staff, children with learning difficulties, or shortage of resources.)

What action will be taken to ensure that these problems are minimised? (ie Who will do what?)

Value implications

In what ways is the innovation congruent with the school's ethos or philosophy?

To what extent are the values implied in or embodied by the innovation consistent with the values implicit in behaviour and practices within the school? (eg staff relationships, management styles, assumptions about human nature, children, teaching and learning.)

In what ways is the innovation congruent with the values, wishes and expectations of students, parents, governors and other interest groups?

What are the possible areas of lack of congruence and how significant are these?

Opportunity costs

All innovations consume resources. These can include finance, space, materials, time, energy and training.

The decision to adopt or implement a particular innovation will mean that certain resources will be allocated to that innovation which could otherwise have been used in other ventures or projects. If this innovation is adopted,

- what other projects may be 'put on the back burner'?
- which staff may be diverted from other projects?
- in what ways may priority lists be affected?
- what further decisions may be pre-empted?

Evaluation evidence

Are there any examples of the same or a similar innovation being successfully adopted elsewhere?

What information about the innovators and their experience is available?

Is there evidence that improvement resulted from the innovation?
What were the improvements?

Were there any problems or difficulties?
What unintended outcomes or side-effects occurred?
How could you avoid or minimise these in your school?

Is it feasible for appropriate staff to see the innovation in action at another school?
Could you use staff from this school as advisers or consultants?

Exploring personal implications of change (EPIC)

> This exercise is designed to enable participants to examine some of the possible impact and consequences of a forthcoming change at the personal level. It consists of a questionnaire to guide users through different aspects of their lives and work which may be affected by a significant innovation, together with suggested ways of using the questionnaire.

This material is adapted from an instrument originally developed as part of a Helios International Development project in South-East Asia.

Aim

The purpose of the EPIC instrument is to enable members of a client system to clarify and share their perceptions of the most significant personal implications of a forthcoming change. When this has been done they are then in a position to decide what should be done in order to manage or cope with the transition.

This process will be important to all those in positions as agents of change, to help them in their role in managing change. It will enable them to monitor staff morale, to ensure that people's perceptions of the likely consequences of change are realistic and to correct any misunderstandings.

Process

Step 1 Organisation members complete the EPIC questionnaire document in relation to their own perceived situation. It is important to allow sufficient time for this to be done thoroughly.

In filling in the different parts of the questionnaire, the first 'response' column should as far as possible have a *factual* base, ie 'In what ways will the new situation be different?' The 'reaction' column can then be used to note one's *feelings* and *judgements* about this aspect of the change, with a summary symbol to be added in the separate column provided as follows:

Summary symbol

+	My reaction to this aspect of the change tends to be positive, or optimistic.
−	My reaction to this aspect of the change tends to be negative, or pessimistic.
?	I am unsure about this aspect: I am neither positive nor negative at the moment.

Step 2 Discussing findings

Alternative A

Participants form review groups of 3 or 4 members. They use the peer counselling method advocated in the earlier SIGMA materials, which is summarised in a section after the EPIC questionnaire.

The emphasis in this method will be on individual adaptation and development, helped by peers.

Alternative B

Participants meet in teams based on work roles to explore the implications of the change together as a group. (This could also be the basis of an ISIS group process feedback exercise – see the first SIGMA Package materials.)

> A meeting should aim to produce a list of key implications to work on. The ultimate purpose would be to channel action to resolve major problems, or enable staff to learn to cope, or come to terms with any which are 'insoluble'.

EPIC – Exploring Personal Implications of Change

This questionnaire is designed to help those involved in any major change to identify significant personal implications in both short-term effects and the long-term issues involved.

It is intended that the results of the completed questionnaire can then be used as the basis for discussion of :

- how clear and valid are our perceptions of the results of change?
- what are the hopes, fears and expectations of those involved?
- what can we do to help us manage the transition?

Participants should complete the questionnaire on their own before initiating discussion of the issues.

In addition to your written responses to the questions, please enter an appropriate sign in the 'Reaction Symbol' box for each response to indicate whether your feelings are positive/optimistic (+), negative/pessimistic (–), or unsure (?) about each issue.

It is suggested that you read through the whole questionnaire first before responding to any of the items.

THE EPIC QUESTIONNAIRE

Issues pertaining to self	*Response*	*Reaction symbol* (+, –, ?)
What will be the effect of the change on your salary?		
How do you think your promotion prospects may be affected?		
How do you see your future?		
How will your formal status be affected?		

Issues pertaining to self (cont)	Response	Reaction symbol (+, −, ?)
How will your image of yourself change?		
In what ways will your key values be affected?		
What will be the consequences in terms of the amount of uncertainty or ambiguity you will have to cope with?		
How will the change enable you to a) use existing strengths? b) build on existing strengths? c) develop new strengths?		
What things will you need to give up?		
Others:		

MANAGING CHANGE AND DEVELOPMENT IN SCHOOLS

Work issues	Response	Reaction symbol (+, −, ?)
How will the nature of your work change?		
How will the balance of your work change?		
How will the volume of work change?		
How will your work change in: – the range of methods you use?		
– the use of resource materials?		
– the knowledge and skill demands?		
– the work pressures and stresses?		
– hours of work?		
– the physical environment?		
– work patterns?		
– the amount of stimulus or challenge?		

Work issues (cont)	Response	Reaction symbol (+, −, ?)
How will the importance of your work change?		☐
How will your work change with regard to: − its visibility?		☐
− your accountability?		☐
− how it will be assessed?		☐
How will your motivation to work and your job satisfaction be affected?		☐
Others:		☐

Relationships with other people	Response	Reaction symbol (+, −, ?)
In what ways do you think your relationships will change: a) with colleagues?		☐
B) with students?		☐

Relationships with other people (cont)	Response	Reaction symbol (+, −, ?)
How will your formal authority be affected: a) with colleagues?		
b) with students?		
Others:		

Summary section

This section should be completed when data from the EPIC questionnaire and the document 'Analysing a projected innovation or change' (pp.117–121 above) have been discussed.

Conclusions

Can you now summarise the arguments for and against the change, taking into account all the data from your analysis?

Your summary should outline the principal benefits expected from adoption of the innovation weighed against *all* the costs which will be incurred.

As part of your summary you should include a synthesis of staff perceptions from the EPIC questionnaire, together with your comments on these.

Decisions

In the light of your conclusions, state and justify your decision on whether you will proceed with adoption of the change and if so what your implementation strategy will be. Possible alternatives include:

Broad front – all or most staff will simultaneously implement the change with effect from a specific date.

Entering wedge – a selected group will implement the change in one part of the school. When this has been successfully accomplished additional members of staff will be involved in the change. Training and support for this 'second wave' of change agents may be provided by members of the pioneer group. This 'entering wedge' process will then continue until the innovation is adopted throughout the school.

Trojan mouse – a very small change agent group (perhaps just one person) will 'try out' a scaled down model or part of the innovation as an experiment over a limited time scale. This will then be used as a demonstration model to convince others of its worth and as a training vehicle for expanding the innovation.

Dandelion clock – all staff will be involved in an In-Service training workshop on the subject of the innovation. The purpose of the workshop will be to inform and educate, and 'hard sell' methods will be avoided. Those who are enthusiastic about the innovation will be encouraged to try it out and be provided with all necessary resources. When this is a demonstrable success resources will be made available for further staff wishing to be involved.

Postpone – put off initiating the change to a later specified date. Use the intervening time well in convincing, preparing and training appropriate people.

Abandon – give up the struggle. This may be for a variety of different reasons: 'It won't work here', 'The costs are too high' or 'We were wrong'.

An innovation checklist: some reminders for the change agent team

Any innovation is a potential threat to the reigning hierarchy of status and power. It can also be a potential threat to the prevailing state of order.

The more fundamental a change is the greater may be the perceived threat to reigning values, to what is defined as 'the known', to safety, security and even professional competence and credibility. This last threat is the hardest to bear for most people: they may have invested many years in developing their knowledge and expertise. Teaching is an art in which the practitioner has little certainty to rely on, and where consequently that which is tried and trusted is not to be cast aside lightly. Yet in any significant innovation the teacher may be expected to volunteer to take up, at least for a time, the burden of increased uncertainty, even temporary incompetence, until the new system is incorporated into the fabric of her work.

The awesome responsibilities of those who have the task of managing change in education should mean the rejection of all haphazard, 'muddling through' approaches to innovation (the 'Dad's Army' method).

It is vital, therefore, when the decision to adopt a significant innovation has been made, to have a checklist of 'reminders' – all the things which one needs to be sure about *before* initiating the change. Once the change is under way, people will be too busy to construct such a checklist. The following questions are intended as an example list of reminders for a management or change agent team. *In responding to each question it is suggested that the user makes a note of what has been done and what the results have been.*

1. Has there been a thorough attempt to identify and assess all the potential stumbling blocks?

2. Have these barriers, and sources of resistance, once identified, been dealt with? Does it now seem that the balance is tipped in favour of the change rather than against it?

3. Does everyone clearly understand what the change involves? (This is especially important in curriculum change: far too often curriculum change does not succeed because people have not fully understood its values, rationale and spirit.)

   The acid test is whether people can explain *in their own words* what they have to do and why it is being done.

4. Have those responsible for managing the change carried out an analysis of what qualities, skills and knowledge are needed to implement the change?

5. Has In-Service training been provided to equip staff with the necessary skills and knowledge?

6. Do all staff involved in the project now possess at least adequate expertise?

7. Have the change management team listed all the materials and other resource requirements necessary for implementation of the change?
(Note – resources include items such as suitable space and adequate time.)

8. Are sufficient resources now readily available and accessible for those who may need them?

9. Has everyone concerned been given a 'bird's eye view' of the innovation, preferably in writing, and setting out:
   - what are the overall goals and specific objectives?
   - how these goals relate to other organisational or curriculum goals?
   - what are the tasks, duties or activities essential to the success of this venture, and how different people's tasks are related and co-ordinated?
   (This could be done by means of a flow diagram or network chart.)

10. Has everyone been made aware of their own specific part in the overall plan, and how their special responsibilities fit in with those in their immediate role set?

11. Has everyone with a responsibility for some aspect of the change made a clear commitment to carry out that responsibility?

12. Has everyone been encouraged to ask questions about every aspect of the change, including the chance to be critical?

13. Have those responsible for management of the change taken heed of questions and concerns, and taken appropriate action?

14. Have arrangements been made on when and how information on the progress of the project will be collected and disseminated?

15. Has everyone been made aware of these arrangements?

16. Have members of staff who may have special difficulty been identified?

17. Is extra support or supervision available for any potentially vulnerable members of staff?

18. Do staff know to whom to go if they need help or advice?

19. Are the existing organisational arrangements compatible with the change? For the change to become fully institutionalised it must be incorporated into the 'steady state' system of the organisation, and sometimes an innovation may create chaos because its impact on the wider system is overlooked.

    Many of the school's everyday practices are taken for granted by staff and over time they seem to become invisible. It is only when a significant change introduces a 'knock-on' effect that the full implications may be realised.